MANAGE
FOR PROFIT,
NOT FOR
MARKET SHARE

MANAGE FOR PROFIT, NOT FOR MARKET SHARE

A Guide to Greater Profits in Highly Contested Markets

Hermann Simon
Frank F. Bilstein
Frank Luby

Harvard Business School Press

Boston, Massachusetts

Library of Congress Cataloging-in-Publication Data
Simon, Hermann.
    Manage for profit, not for market share : a guide to greater profits in highly
contested markets / Hermann Simon, Frank F. Bilstein, and Frank Luby.
        p. cm.
    Includes bibliographical references.
    ISBN 1-59139-526-7 (perm. paper)
    1. Profit. 2. Profit—Case studies. 3. Industrial management—Case studies.
I. Bilstein, Frank F., 1971– II. Luby, Frank, 1964– III. Title.
HB601.S56 2006
658.15'5—dc22

                                                        2005037019

The paper used in this publication meets the minimum requirements of the American National Standard for Information Sciences—Permanence of Paper for
Printed Library Materials, ANSI Z39.48-1992.

In memory of Peter Drucker

Contents

CHAPTER 1

Choose Profit over Market Share

We need to free ourselves from this market share mania. Market share should be a means to an end, and not the end itself.
—CEO of a global market leader

To FIND the most potent symbol of distress in contemporary business management, you need not comb through Chapter 11 filings or the testimony at a high-profile fraud trial. Instead, you could examine photographs of some middle-aged executives from Michigan to find a small fashion accessory: an embossed lapel pin shaped as the number 29.[1]

Senior executives at General Motors Corporation did not wear these pins to commemorate an anniversary, an engine size, or the number of new model launches. The pin underscored their commitment to a performance target in the highly competitive North American market. General Motors wanted a North American market share of 29 percent and focused all of its resources to achieve it. When the company fell short of the target, some managers continued to wear the pin anyway.

"'29' will be there until we hit '29'," said Gary Cowger, president of GM North America, in an interview in 2004. "And then I'll probably buy a '30'."[2]

We respect and admire these managers' ability to motivate such a sprawling organization around one simple target and remain devoted to that target despite setbacks. That is not an easy task. But we count the GM executives among the more prominent victims of a misconception that may be as old as management thinking itself. The misconception is the fiercely held belief that market share is the most appropriate basis for setting corporate goals, managing the corporation, and measuring its performance. The "29" pin at General Motors is just one example of the overwhelming and enduring influence this belief can exert on the culture of a company.

This book marks a clear break with the traditions and teachings that have turned the belief in the limitless power of market share into today's greatest management fallacy. In this book, we will expose the inherent contradictions and destructive impact of the market share obsession, and call for managers to make a renewed and forceful commitment to profit. We call for a profit renaissance, led by companies in highly contested markets who have learned how to redirect all of their marketing efforts—pricing, product, positioning, and promotion—toward earning more money rather than selling greater volumes.

For decades, managers have heard incessantly from colleagues, superiors, professors, and pundits that their salvation lies in pursuing and preserving high market share. Consequently, they built every aspect of their organization, from strategy and sales to marketing and manufacturing, to achieve that goal. Training sessions, incentives systems, and war stories from other industries helped strengthen their resolve.

Rewarded by their superiors and their boards of directors for their market share achievements, managers rarely questioned whether they might better serve their company and their own career ambitions by doing the unthinkable: abandoning market share as their company's guiding principle for growth. What's wrong with market share as a guiding principle for strategy? It's hard to know where to begin. Its definition is arbitrary and often misleading. When companies make it the centerpiece of their "profitable growth" strategies, it gives rise to cultures and behaviors that destroy profit rather than boost it.

Our call would ring hollow if we could not back up our claims and provide a program for change. We argue that companies in any mature market—not just the automotive industry—that let market share or sales volume guide their actions will fall well short of their earnings potential. In fact, the profits these managers sacrifice amount to 1 to 3 percent of their company's annual revenue. Simply put, that means the manager of a $5 billion business leaves between $50 million and $150 million in his customers' and competitors' pockets every year as long as he clings to the outdated market share dogma. This figure is neither a coincidence nor a theoretical estimate drawn on some blackboard or crunched on a supercomputer. It derives from the real-life revenue-driven turnarounds that hundreds of companies have achieved and that form the basis for most of the stories and case examples in this book.

For some companies, the program for change meant more than additional profits; it meant survival. Undertaking the program prevented these companies from taking strategic missteps whose consequences—usually unforeseen and massive—would have likely started or accelerated their demise.

Armed with evidence drawn from our extensive management consulting experience, we feel we can achieve two objectives with this book. First, we want to convince you to make profit your primary goal and reinforce that commitment. Then we want you to bring your company closer to peak profit performance by undertaking the practical, proven program that forms the bulk of this book. That will require courage and patience, but the rewards certainly justify the effort.

The program is not designed for the thrill-seeking executive who is out to change the world and turn his industry upside down. We aim it at the managers and executives in mature markets who would like to replace adrenaline with analysis, and replace dogma with detail and evidence, to improve their companies' profits. This program may not earn you an action-figure nickname like Chainsaw Al or Neutron Jack. But it will earn your company much more money.

We will devote the first two-thirds of this introductory chapter to the profit and marketing malaise that has taken hold of managers in mature markets. The final third of the chapter will give an initial overview of how managers can overcome that malaise, step by step, by following our program.

Recognize the Symptoms of the Profit Malaise

Ask the person on the street how much profit a typical company earns on $100 in sales, and most answers will fall between 25 and 50 percent.[3] Nothing could be further from the truth. The real aggregate profit margins of companies in most developed industrial countries lie dangerously close to zero.[4] Figure 1-1 shows the after-tax profit margins of internationally active manufacturing companies in nineteen countries.

Well-known phenomena such as global competition, overcapacity, and sluggish or declining demand help explain these depressing results. These factors will endure, if not intensify, in the coming years. One individual company would have difficulty influencing these external trends. Therefore, most companies in highly developed economies will continue to have a serious problem in turning a reasonable profit, unless they take action within their own organizations.

What are their reasonable options? Managers undertake three initiatives, usually in parallel. They cut costs, invest in innovation, and change their marketing. Cost cutting is the most obvious and

4

FIGURE 1-1

After-tax margins exceed 5 percent only in smaller industrialized economies.

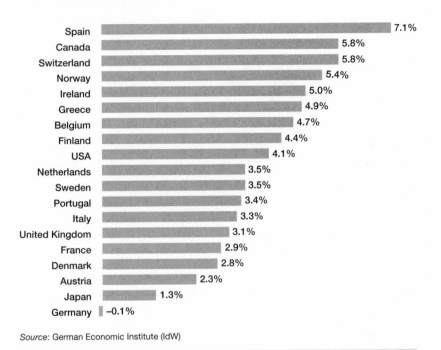

Spain	7.1%
Canada	5.8%
Switzerland	5.8%
Norway	5.4%
Ireland	5.0%
Greece	4.9%
Belgium	4.7%
Finland	4.4%
USA	4.1%
Netherlands	3.5%
Sweden	3.5%
Portugal	3.4%
Italy	3.3%
United Kingdom	3.1%
France	2.9%
Denmark	2.8%
Austria	2.3%
Japan	1.3%
Germany	–0.1%

Source: German Economic Institute (IdW)

widely practiced of the three options because it provides the most immediate benefits. You will find plenty of books to help you do this properly, so we will not explore cost cutting in detail in this book. We will, however, raise a critical question for many managers: what happens when cost cutting has reached its limits as a source of profit growth? In other words, how should a company respond when it and its competitors have achieved similar levels of productivity and enjoy roughly similar cost structures? A marketing vice president at a manufacturing company put this problem in context for us: "Our products have few advantages anymore. You could probably call them commodities," he explained. "Competition is clobbering us, customers have put us under enormous pressure, and we've done all we can on the cost side. What can I do about this? What options do I have to get higher profits?"

Innovation, like cost cutting, is an essential and continual task for any company. No one disputes that managers face the constant challenge to innovate to maintain or accelerate the company's revenue and profit growth, and thus escape from the cost and price pressures of the real world. There is just one major problem with this approach: innovation pipelines rarely offer just-in-time delivery. The dream of the big breakthrough—and the near monopoly status and pioneer returns that accompany it—remains just that, a dream. Creative business models, which are just as rare as product and service innovations, require years to take hold and offer no guarantee of success.

A sales manager at a multibillion-dollar global manufacturer summed this up by saying that "all this stuff I hear about 'being innovative' is fine. But the products I'm selling are at least ten years old, and no one's going to hand me an innovation tomorrow morning. So what am I supposed to do in the meantime?"

As with cost cutting, bookshelves overflow with guidance on how to manage innovation. This book does not serve as a replacement for this type of strategic guidance, but instead serves managers in mature markets, who cannot afford to wait for a mythical breakthrough product. These managers are acutely aware that the following five conditions apply to them and their competitors:

- They have made all sensible gains from cost cutting.

- Most of their revenue and profit will continue to come from established products with relatively flat market growth.

- The unique edge of most of their products has eroded.

- Competition is fierce.

- Customers can switch suppliers easily.

These conditions give rise to two fundamental contradictions. First, one would expect that once a company has carved out a profitable market position, it could continue to grow its profits by expanding that market position—that is, by increasing its market share. That is what the Profit Impact of Marketing Strategy (PIMS) study and the experience curve concept teach. Yet the insights and case examples throughout this book will show that this expectation is at best dangerous, at worst outright wrong, when a company competes in a mature market.

Second, one would expect the financial performance of competitors to remain broadly similar and consistent, because they all produce the same products with the same cost structures and compete for the same customers. Our case examples show that this does not hold true in mature markets. Lacking the ability to obtain a sustainable cost advantage or launch an innovation, managers have no choice but to gain an advantage by improving the quality of their revenue. Superior performers make more sophisticated use of their marketing mix to generate revenue from customers with the highest profit potential, and not just revenue for revenue's sake. The cases in this book will demonstrate two crucial points:

- Better revenue quality and growth, derived from better use of their marketing capabilities, is often the sole explanation between average and superior profit performance.

- The superior performers have stopped using market share as a means to set goals and measure success. They have focused instead on profit.

We dedicate this book, then, to the forgotten stepchildren in companies around the world, the mature products that generate the bulk of company sales and "keep the lights turned on." We know from our consulting practice that they bear a huge profit potential that managers have either ignored or struggled to tap. Innovation and cost cutting will not unlock that potential. You must change two things to increase your profits by the equivalent of 1 to 3 percent of your annual revenue. You must abandon the market share mind-set in favor of a profit-oriented one, and you must change the way you generate revenue by following the program laid out in chapters 2 through 10.

Appreciate Why Market Share Dominates Managerial Thinking

Where did this management fascination with market share come from? It has many roots. We would like to explain the legitimate origins of the link between market share and profit, how initial enthusiasm over this link grew into a management fascination, and how an overly simplistic interpretation of the original findings can lead to dangerous and destructive decisions for managers competing in highly contested markets.

The most widely known root of the market share movement is the PIMS study, whose most important finding we show in figure 1-2.[5]

Regardless of whether one defines market share by rank or percentage, there is a strong and highly significant correlation between market share and profit margin. The market leader enjoys a profit margin, measured in the PIMS study as pretax return on investment, that is roughly three times as high as the margin the fifth-largest competitor earns. A supplier with a market share of 40 percent will achieve a margin twice as high as the competitor with just 10 percent of the market. The strategic implication could not seem more clear or straightforward: Get market share! Long live economies of scale!

A second, slightly older source behind the market share movement is the experience curve. This concept says that a company's cost position depends on its relative market share. A company's relative market share equals its own share divided by the share of its

FIGURE 1-2

PIMS showed the correlation between market share and profit

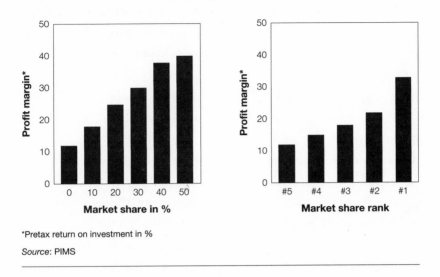

*Pretax return on investment in %

Source: PIMS

strongest competitor. The higher this number is, the lower that company's unit costs should be.[6] The market leader automatically has the lowest costs in the market and therefore the highest profit margin. The experience curve effect formed the basis for the famous two-by-two portfolio matrix, or "Boston" matrix, with the dimensions "market growth" and "relative market share." Each of the four resulting matrix spaces called for a different ideal strategy with the management of market share as the centerpiece. Once again, the strategic implication is clear: a company is best off when it drives its market share as high as possible.

The experience curve and the PIMS study are the grandparents of all market share philosophies. Former General Electric chairman and CEO Jack Welch became their most famous advocate in the early 1980s when he insisted that his company would exit any business in which it did not hold the number one or number two position.

9

Interestingly, some subsequent studies questioned the strict relationship between market share and margin. They uncovered a much weaker relationship between market share and profit than the PIMS authors did.[7] The deconstruction of the original findings continues to this day. An anthology edited and published in the year 2003 by Paul W. Farris and Michael J. Moore provides the latest views.[8] The most important question is whether the relationship between market share and profit represents a true causal relationship or a mere correlation. Support has increased for the latter hypothesis. Researchers who have applied modern analytical methods to filter out the effects of so-called unobserved factors, have concluded that "once the impact of these unobserved factors is econometrically removed, the remaining effect of market share on profitability is quite small."[9] The authors do conclude that "although high market share, by itself, does not increase profitability, it does enable high share firms to take certain profitable actions that may not be feasible for low share firms."[10] That conclusion does not refute PIMS or the experience curve outright, nor does it give justification to say Jack Welch was wrong. But it certainly calls the universal application and relevance of the "market share is everything" philosophy into question.

While those authors directly challenge the PIMS conclusions, others have taken a broader look at the influence of competitor-oriented goals such as market share or market position. The earliest prominent findings predate both PIMS and Jack Welch's tenure at General Electric. In 1958, Robert F. Lanzillotti showed a negative correlation between the commitment to competitor-oriented objectives (such as market share) and a company's return on investment.[11] A recent paper by J. Scott Armstrong and Kesten C. Green summarizes some additional recent evidence and concludes that ". . . competitor-oriented objectives are harmful. However, this evidence has had only a modest impact on academic research and it seems to be largely ignored by managers."[12] These papers are just two of many studies, which have attempted to measure the effects of market share or market position goals, the experience curve, and portfolio management guided by the so-called Boston Matrix. Taken together, the breadth and mass of evidence leads to one clear conclusion: an unwavering organizational commitment to competitor-oriented goals, the tools that underpin them, and the behaviors they encourage will harm a company's ability to earn profits in a highly contested (mature) market.

Why do a company's management and its investors nonetheless continue to buy into this "market share is everything" philosophy? The answer is simple: market share, volume, and revenue growth are the best indicators of truly sustainable success through innovation. When a company conquers a market as Starbucks has done in coffee, observers intuitively assume that continued market share growth is good. It suggests superiority, which in turn suggests sustainable profits. Starbucks deserves the growth it has enjoyed and the returns it has achieved. When a company has an innovative product or other clear competitive advantages, a market share–driven approach is fine.

But Starbucks' competitive situation has already begun to change. Dunkin' Donuts, Krispy Kreme, McDonald's, and even the gasoline station on the corner have begun installing espresso machines and offering their own range of drinks. As this market continues to mature, how much longer will Starbucks deserve the market share growth when it no longer has its sustainable superiority?

The company's mission statement lists "Recognize that profitability is essential to our future success" as one of six guiding principles.[13] But the company's public filings make the current strategy clear, at least for the retail stores: "Starbucks strategy for expanding its retail business is to increase its market share in existing markets primarily by opening additional stores and to open stores in new markets where the opportunity exists to become the leading specialty coffee retailer."[14]

At some point, the same five conditions of mature markets, listed earlier, will apply to Starbucks and its competitors. When that day comes, the company will need to abandon its anchor to market share and reorient itself around profit to preserve its premium position and the profits it allows. We will revisit this issue in chapter 2 when we introduced the concept of competition maps, using Starbucks and its competitors as an example.

In highly contested markets, managers see a much different landscape than Starbucks has enjoyed thus far. Overall volume is roughly constant. Marketing efforts from competitors often have little or no impact on boosting overall demand. Price cuts—within realistic limits—shift sales from one competitor to another but likewise have little effect on overall demand. Market shares, however, can undergo significant shifts, depending on how aggressively the various competitors behave.

The formula shown in figure 1-3 offers some additional insight into how managers view market share.

If market volume totals $1 billion, a company with a 10 percent market share and 10 percent margin will have revenue of $100 million and a profit of $10 million. Expanding the market size is difficult in mature markets. An individual firm can do little in this regard. Expanding margins offers more promise. Margin is the difference

FIGURE 1-3

Additional insight into how managers view market share

Source: Simon-Kucher & Partners

between unit price and unit cost. Cost cuts would make a direct and complete contribution to higher margins, but as we said before, most companies in mature markets have already made most or all of their reasonable cost cuts. This leaves pricing as a highly effective and often neglected profit driver that we will spend much of this book elaborating on.

Any increase in market share would have a linear (and thus strong) effect on profit. If the company we just described doubled its market share from 10 percent to 20 percent, it would double its profit. An individual company may not be able to influence overall market volume, but it can certainly influence its own market share through a variety of initiatives. These can include additional advertising, sales force expansion, promotions, and price as well. This representation may be somewhat oversimplified, but market share tempts managers as a Pandora's box for solving their profit problems, because they focus on revenue for revenue's sake, rather than using these very same initiatives to increase their profits.

Adding to the temptation is the crude application of the PIMS and experience curve lessons to this equation. If you truly believe that higher market share leads to higher margins, you will have discovered the wonder drug for any company facing a profit problem. Let's say that a company increases its market share from 10 percent to 20 percent, resulting in a margin increase from 10 percent to 20 percent. In our example, profit would expand geometrically, not linearly, to $40 million, which would be a fantastic, historic achievement. Our cases will demonstrate that it is also a rather unrealistic one. In mature markets, where the PIMS logic starts to fall apart, incremental gains in market share usually have a disproportionately *negative* effect on profit. The irony is that the harder a company pursues and defends this approach, the more it destroys its own profit potential.[15]

Make a Clean Break with the Market Share Culture

The heading of this section is easier said than done. While academic researchers toiled behind the scenes to test the PIMS hypotheses further, business schools initiated thousands of MBA students into the market share cult. Those who earned their MBA degrees in the 1970s and 1980s—and who soaked up the philosophy in its freshest, most concentrated form—now hold C-level positions. The crowning moment in the spread of market share fascination came with the Internet wave. In the years of Internet and e-business hype, the only metrics that mattered were sales growth, market position, market share, and the absolute number of customers. Had you dared to breathe the word *profit*, managers would have stigmatized you as "old economy."

The Internet bubble popped, but don't believe that it also washed away managers' memories. Many of these misguided pursuits—such as more market share, more customers, and more revenue growth—have not only remained in place, they have become entrenched. Anyone who loses market share—or even considers doing something that puts it at risk—is asking for serious trouble in most companies. You can expect a sharp, even malicious response from the press, analysts, shareholders, your colleagues, and even local authorities if you make this suggestion.

We witnessed this problem firsthand at a premium automobile manufacturer we'll call United Motors Corporation (UMC) for short.[16] The company's head of sales noted with resignation that "when we are honest with ourselves, it's clear that we just pay lip service to profit goals and targets. If our profit falls by 20 percent, nothing happens. If our market share falls by even a fraction of a percentage point, heads roll. And everybody knows it."

The same undercurrent ran through a presentation we made at the headquarters of an Asian consumer electronics company, whose pretax profit margin consistently came in under 5 percent in recent years.[17] The company could not blame the performance on global competition and price pressures when its leading competitor, Samsung Electronics, earned a pretax margin of over 15 percent. In the course of the discussion, it became clear that this company could best improve its margins quickly by raising prices and scaling back its generous discount and rebate programs with retailers.

"But that would mean we would lose market share," one manager said. The room went silent. We had touched a taboo subject. An intentional loss of market share would be unthinkable for most Asian companies, even if the company earned higher profits.

We know from our experience that no one enjoys losing market share. We risk making enemies at the start of a consulting project when we raise the possibility, even implicitly. One client, in fact, told us straight up in our first meeting that "if your recommendations mean we will end up losing market share, don't bother buying a plane ticket back down here."

Market share remains a widespread and influential performance indicator, internally and externally. Successfully making the mental shift from a market share focus to a profit one involves overcoming not just philosophical resistance, but cultural resistance as well. Companies that have relentlessly pursued market share growth or preservation inevitably have one of two entrenched corporate cultures: aggression or acquiescence.

The culture of outright aggressiveness in the marketplace is more common. Overly ambitious market share goals—often combined with a neglect of profit orientation—induce aggressive actions that in turn provoke equally or even more aggressive reactions by the competitors. U.S.-based carmakers embarked on this path in the summer of 2005, when Ford and DaimlerChrysler felt compelled to match General Motors' "employee discount" program with even more attractive, similarly named programs of their own.

A culture of aggression within mature markets spawns price wars and profit destruction on a grand scale. Fortunately, a growing number of recent management books condemn this kind of aggressiveness. Notable is the best-selling and widely praised *Blue Ocean Strategy.*[18] While this book—in contrast to ours—focuses primarily on new products and new business models, it contains a similar message: that peaceful competition is a reasonable, rational form of behavior.

Openly aggressive companies take destructive actions to gain share from competitors, while acquiescent ones take destructive actions to preserve market share positions. These companies train their sales and marketing teams to make concessions (better value, lower prices) whenever the customer makes a threat to take business elsewhere. The compulsion to hit a market share or volume target leads them to surrender to demanding customers, who often determine the course of negotiations and set the terms themselves. A culture of acquiescence results when a company does whatever it takes to retain business. The ultimate sin in this culture is to lose a customer and, thus, market share. In this case, companies essentially cede strategic control of their business to their customers, who gain the prices, terms, and conditions they want. Even when managers know that customers might be taking advantage of them in this manner, they feel reluctant or even powerless to change the situation.

A culture of acquiescence is most common in industries with large, concentrated customers, such as the relationships between automakers and their suppliers or between national retailers (Wal-Mart, Target) and their suppliers. But we also observe these cultures in service industries such as telecommunications, banking, or software, where parties negotiate most of their transaction prices and sales teams enjoy liberal negotiating leeway. Customers can essentially dictate their own conditions because the supplier fears antagonizing them or ultimately losing the business.

What escapes these companies is that their acquiescence can have the same caustic effects on profit as an open war against the competition, but without the colorful military metaphors and public hoopla. Each time a company's sales or management team surrenders to customer pressure, it creates three unintended effects that will haunt it in its subsequent dealings. First, it has allowed the customer to demand and receive better value at lower prices. Thus, it has redefined the prevailing standards for value and price. These become the basis for the next negotiation, in which any savvy customer will most certainly want to widen the gulf even further between value and price. Second, the company has earned itself a reputation as a nice guy or a soft touch. Third, the damage the company has done to price-value relationships in its market allows customers to add credibility to their threats at other suppliers. The cycle perpetuates itself.

One should not underestimate the role that senior management's attitude plays in reinforcing these cultures. Think back to the example of the "29" lapel pin at the start of this chapter. In their article "Primal Leadership: The Hidden Driver of Great Performance," authors Daniel Goleman, Richard Boyatzis, and Annie McKee point out how managers' behavior directly impacts the whole organization.[19] People will read and interpret senior management's nonverbal signals, regardless of what those managers tell them explicitly about their goals. The problems start when these goals—both explicit and implicit—do not match.

The next section of this introductory chapter describes the change program we have helped companies customize and implement. Our body of evidence derives primarily from our experience in helping over five hundred companies around the world increase their profits under the confining, often disillusioning conditions that a mature marketplace seems to impose on them. That experience has shown us how much additional profit companies can achieve if they abandon their aggressive or acquiescent approaches in favor of a profit-oriented culture. It has also revealed what resources managers require to pursue the program in this book, and why they can expect a rapid payback if they remain true to it. Most of our projects are highly confidential. A company trying to wring more money from its dealings as a supplier to Wal-Mart or General Motors does not want these activities to become common knowledge. To respect client confidentiality we have disguised the facts and often the industry in each case example, because they derive from an inside perspective, not from publicly available information.

Learn How to Focus Your Marketing Efforts on Profit

The methods and techniques described in this book address the revenue side of your business. We are not cost cutters. True to the maxim "Stick to your knitting," we knew that it would make no sense for us to write a book about cost cutting, rationalization, or efficiency improvements. The key issue resolved in this book is, How does a manager in a mature market alter his or her marketing mix to achieve better revenue quality and thus a sustainable increase in profit?

Cost cutting and productivity improvement efforts have certainly succeeded per se over the last twenty years, and yet the profit malaise endures, as figure 1-1 showed. Companies now must apply the same energy, intelligence, and commitment to the customer-facing side of their businesses. As we've said before, managers have barely begun to identify and tap this large profit opportunity.

Figure 1-4 shows the kinds of increased margins and absolute profits companies have achieved by actively identifying and seizing profit opportunities by using the integrated program we reveal in this book. The margin and profit improvements represent the difference (in percentage points and in absolute dollars) between "as usual" profit performance and peak profit performance.

FIGURE 1-4

The profit improvements are real, not theoretical

Industry	Company revenue (US$)	Profit increase (as percentage of revenue)
Industrial supplier	5–10 billion	1.2
Construction	< 1 billion	1.1
Engineering	5–10 billion	1.0
Wholesaler	1–5 billion	2.0
Banking	1–5 billion	1.6
Tourism	5–10 billion	1.6
Express delivery	5–10 billion	1.5
Software	100–500 million	3.0

Source: Consulting projects conducted by Simon-Kucher & Partners

Finding and tapping your profit opportunities requires an integrated program that thrives on straightforward, nose-to-the-grindstone problem solving, not splash and sizzle. The work the companies in our cases undertook is not rocket science, but it is arduous. Unfortunately, there is no magical "fix this and you're done" approach to earning this additional profit. This book will provide you with the guidance and tools, but you still must make the commitment and effort to find and retrieve all that money, dollar by dollar. Fortunately, the magnitude of the changes you must make is less radical than you might imagine.

Our proven program has four phases, as shown in figure 1-5. The first phase—covered in chapters 2 and 3—focuses on changing your mind-set by showing you alternatives to the destructive cultures of aggression and acquiescence. These two chapters will help you understand and resolve your goal conflicts, place more emphasis on profit, and add discipline and rigor to your marketing and sales efforts.

FIGURE 1-5

Our four-phase program for finding and extracting higher profits from your market

Phase 1 Change your mind-set	Chapter 2 Learn to compete peacefully	Chapter 3 Change the way you form assumptions
Phase 2 Get the right data and information	Chapter 4 Use internal data to find profit opportunities	Chapter 5 Uncover preferences and willingness to pay
Phase 3 Pursue your profit opportunities	Chapters 6 and 7 Optimize your marketing mix	Chapter 8 Don't ingratiate yourself with customers
Phase 4 Protect your profit	Chapter 9 Align your incentives to focus on profit	Chapter 10 Get your market communication under control

Source: Simon-Kucher & Partners

The goal of chapter 2 is to show you how you can extend the life span and the profitability of your mature products. This demands that you do four things:

- Strive for differentiation.

- Pick your fights intelligently.

- Concede market share that you can't hold profitably.

- Resist the temptation to slash prices when aggressors threaten your business.

The thrill seekers in your market—and right now you may even be one of them!—do none of this. They respond to any attack with a counterattack, a price cut with a price cut, and product proliferation with product proliferation, often without ever considering an alternative or weighing the long-term consequences.

No longer willing to differentiate their products or replace them quickly with new ones, aggressive managers wield price as their lone differentiating factor. Consequently, their salespeople spend more time getting management's permission to charge lower prices than building customer relationships at higher prices. Underlying these situations is an unctuous marketing malaise throughout the company. Aggressors reduce the elements of the marketing mix to crude, blunt instruments with which they can pummel the competition or grovel before customers.

It follows, then, that you must find the open-minded people in your organization and convert as many aggressive colleagues as possible to rally behind the banner of profit. Most companies we have worked with succeeded on both counts.

Chapter 3 will show you how to shatter the specific pieces of conventional wisdom that have led you to overlook the sources of additional profit. The chapter explains the dangers inherent in using gut feeling, anecdotal evidence, and other corporate shortcuts to guide your decision making. Then it uses the link between price and profit to demonstrate the advantages of data-driven analysis. Knowing what math to do, then "doing the math" consistently, marks a major step forward. This step is especially relevant for companies with a culture of acquiescence. Learning to base your decisions on thorough analysis will help you to take the emotion out of decision making and resist customer demands.

The second phase of the program (chapters 4 and 5) defines and describes the data and information you will need to make objective marketing decisions. You will probably agree that chapters 2 and 3 foster the desire to make marketing decisions based on facts and evidence, rather than gut feeling. But you will only accomplish this if you can actually produce the right facts and evidence and make them readily available within your organization. Without that transparency, you cannot identify the extent of your additional profit opportunities. Most companies face a big challenge in achieving the right transparency in their marketing data. The data and information on the sales and marketing side rarely exists in a comparable level of detail as on the cost side, where a CFO or finance director can readily access relevant information.

Chapter 4 shows you how to organize your internal data and then extract new insights from this data. These insights will help you identify how you can differentiate your product and service offerings, how you can repair and reinforce their price-value relationships by doing the math, and how you can determine how much more your company should be earning. Chapter 5 has a similar objective, but focuses on external market research rather than your internal data. It shows how you can gain a sharper understanding of your customers' preferences to shift more money from their pockets to yours.

After the first two phases, you will have outfitted yourself with the right mind-set, data, and information. You should have a very good idea of where your unexploited profit opportunities are and how much you can expect to find. Now it's time to start earning the money. The third phase (chapters 6 through 8) will show you how to apply what you've learned to restore the subtlety and sophistication to your marketing mix.

Chapter 6 addresses place, product, and promotion. It offers you alternative ways to segment your customers according to their preferences and to configure the right product and service packages for them. In this chapter, you begin to see clearly how you can capture additional profits from the same products and services you have right now. The difference is that you have changed how you combine them and how you select your targets for them. Chapter 6 also stresses the importance of timing your promotional activities properly, to generate the highest profits and keep the greatest share of these profits for yourself.

Chapter 7 has one central theme: how to raise your prices. It operates on the premise that you have identified and quantified your additional profit potential, and now you must go out and earn it. In some, rather specific cases, lower prices, higher discounts, or other increases in customer incentives do contribute to higher profits. But these situations seldom arise in highly contested markets. When we say "raising prices," we don't mean that you should simply tack on a few percentage points to every price, across the board. Price increases can take many forms, ranging from a direct increase to lower discounts, a lower level of service, a change in your pricing structure, or more restrictive financial terms.

To provide a cross-check on your enthusiasm, chapter 8 takes a close look at the risks you run in changing your marketing mix. Despite the progress you have made with the program thus far, you will always face the alluring temptation to revert to old habits and become overly generous to your customers. That old specter of market share will tempt you to go after a few extra customers by sacrificing margins, fattening up cumbersome loyalty programs, or sweetening deals for customers with services they are not willing to pay for. Chapter 8 sounds a warning against those risks.

The final phase (chapters 9 and 10) covers two critical issues that will help you make your actions deliver sustainable profit, not just a one-off boost. Recall that our program usually allows you to capture your substantial profit opportunities with the same people you already have, not just the same products. Clearly, you will jeopardize your chances if your sales and marketing teams do not support your efforts and participate in them. Critical in ensuring their compliance is your incentive system, the subject of chapter 9. Too often we find companies who claim to pursue higher profits, but still reward their salespeople for achieving aggressive, pure volume or pure revenue targets. Aligning incentives with corporate goals is essential. These incentives include cash compensation, which should emphasize profit rather than revenue or volume. But they also include softer status incentives. If you want an organization of open-minded, evidence-oriented people, reward those people. If you want an organization of aggressors, reward aggressors. The problem is that many organizations try to abandon aggressive behavior, but still encourage it because they leave their outdated volume-driven incentive systems in place.

In chapter 10 we offer advice to help you understand the consequences of your actions in the marketplace, and what steps you can take to minimize the risk of unfavorable outcomes. We will show you how to control all facets of your market communication. As your profits begin to grow, the market will watch you with keen interest. Your actions should serve to prevent uncertainty in the market. The same applies to what you and your colleagues say publicly. Inconsistent communication to the market can be a catastrophic strategic mistake. In a climate of uncertainty, you can never predict in advance how customers, investors, or competitors might respond, nor can you estimate the damage their responses might do to your profits. Don't let them undermine your efforts. Clear actions and communication—within legal limits—will help you mitigate that risk.

The preceding introduction to the individual chapters may tempt you to cherry-pick, because one or two chapters may have more relevance than others for an urgent issue you currently face. We will not discourage you from doing so, but we would like to stress that the full extent of your profit opportunities emerges when you pursue the entire program, not just the most immediate and compelling aspect for your company. The program is holistic, not a haphazard collection of discrete ideas and approaches.

To illustrate this point, let's assume you jump to chapter 7 right away because you are planning a price increase and would like some guidance or some confirmation for your decision. The cases and discussion in chapter 7 should provide you with the insight on how to raise prices effectively and also give you the confidence and cover to execute the changes. But we would consider such a move in isolation to be somewhat risky—even reckless, depending on your market—unless you have also figured out the entire picture. You must understand how your competitors might respond and what countermoves you might need (chapter 2), and make sure you have taken a close look at your link between your marketing instruments, market share, and profit (chapter 3). Have you found the data to let you pinpoint the precise magnitude of the necessary changes and the profit at stake (chapters 4 and 5)? Have you determined how to target the price increase properly and which products and services it should apply to (chapter 6)? Have you eliminated ways to undermine the decision (chapter 8)? Have you aligned your incentives to ensure that your sales team pushes the desired actions through instead of ignoring them (chapter 9)? Have you determined how you will speak and act publicly in a clear, consistent manner (chapter 10)?

Chapter 11 summarizes our findings and recommendations and gives additional advice for implementation and leadership.

Summary

The profit malaise is pandemic. Many companies have exhausted their potential for cost savings and have no innovations on the way. This means they must turn their attention to the mature products to improve their profits. This book, therefore, focuses on higher profits by improving the revenue quality of mature products, not by cutting costs or investing in innovation.

What prevents companies from addressing this need is the misguided yet widely held belief born in the 1970s and preached to thousands of managers around the world: the power of market share as a profit driver. A cultural shift is long overdue. In this book, we challenge this market share creed and offer a more profitable alternative.

The key issue resolved in this book is, How does a manager in a highly contested market achieve a sustainable increase in profit without cost cutting or innovation? Our first step is to make the market share–versus–profit dilemma clear by explaining the conditions under which certain strategies will work and won't work. By recognizing this and adjusting goals accordingly, managers can take a first step in eradicating the dangerous cultures of aggression and acquiescence that have grown up in the wake of the market share obsession.

Our recommendations derive from three premises, based on our consulting and research experience. First, you can extract a huge profit potential—equivalent to 1 to 3 percent of revenue—by pursuing a profit orientation instead of a market share one. Second, you can implement the program in this book quickly and affordably by relying on your currently available resources and without firing people or initiating costly, long-term innovation efforts. Third, this program requires many small but powerful steps rather than one big thing.

We would like to make one final remark before you embark on your reorientation. You will find the task much easier if you pursue it without assigning blame. Why no one noticed these profit opportunities before—or bothered to search for them—would be a topic for an interesting but ultimately useless discussion. Often there is no clear root cause to explain why the profit opportunities remained hidden and unexploited for so long. Please keep your eye on the vast windfall that the additional profit promises, rather than dwelling on the past.

CHAPTER 2

Learn to Compete Peacefully

Never will a man penetrate deeper into error than when he is
continuing on a road that has led him to great success.
—Friedrich von Hayek[1]

G IVEN THE PASSION most managers bring to their work, it is easy to forget that business is not warfare. Business and war differ in two critical aspects: first, war always ends, but competition never does; second, there are no customers on a military battlefield. Military missions have very little in common with what you do in your business on a daily basis. You are trying to attract and keep customers, not capture fugitives or disable opponents. You should not require a few chapters of Sun Tzu or a piece of juicy competitive intelligence to spur you into action every morning. Business is not a covert operation.

If you think that sounds like a plea for peaceful competition in markets, you are correct. In the absence of breakthrough innovations, peaceful competitors strive to extend the life span and profitability of their established products. They differentiate products to match up with customer preferences and concentrate on profitable customer segments, even if that means ceding market share to competitors in areas where they are not strong enough.

Identify the Aggressors in Your Market

Recall the critical issue we mentioned in the first chapter: the philosophical tug-of-war between increasing your market share and increasing your profit. Aggressive and acquiescent companies fear the loss of volume (and thus market share), so they build their entire marketing strategy around preserving or even increasing it. Customers learn to take advantage of a company's aggressiveness or willingness to give in, which compounds the downward pressure on profit. Peaceful competitors build an entire market strategy around preserving or increasing *profit*. They refuse to see themselves locked in a zero-sum competition for market share, which fosters a "kill or be killed" mentality. They would rather be different than be the ultimate "winner."

When this approach is taken to the extreme, aggressive or acquiescent managers actually consider their mind-sets to be defensive. They become trapped in the vicious cycle shown in figure 2-1. Like former Green Beret John Rambo in the first film of that eponymous series, they defend their actions in the marketplace by repeating that

FIGURE 2-1

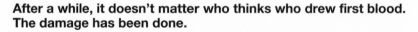

After a while, it doesn't matter who thinks who drew first blood. The damage has been done.

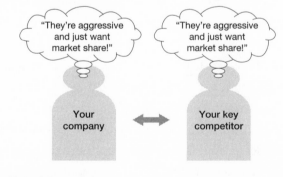

Source: Simon-Kucher & Partners

"they drew first blood. Not me." The adrenaline rush of competition makes it hard for some managers to renounce business strategies based on market share or volume. The cases later in this chapter will show how companies either have succeeded in renouncing it or have avoided the trap altogether.

At a valve manufacturer, most of the company's senior staff regarded their mature product lines as commodities. We'll call this company Freshwater. Rapid penetration of the U.S. market had turned it from a regional leader to a global powerhouse. The management group that built up that presence now had overall control of the company. While the group proclaimed a new strategy of "profitable growth," their "volume at all costs" attitude lurked just below the surface.[2]

CASE STUDY

Issue: How to Rein in Aggressive Behavior

Company: Freshwater Industries
Product: Valves
Source: Simon-Kucher & Partners project

Freshwater's plan for the next two years was simple: attack. It felt that its staunchest competitor, likewise a global player, would soon launch a price war. If Freshwater moved first, it could put this "very aggressive, unpredictable" competitor—we'll call it Algonquin Manufacturing—on the defensive and steal a few points of market share from it. As a first step in trying to convince Freshwater's managers to reconsider this strategy, we asked them to prove that their competitor was really aggressive. What evidence did they have?

Freshwater's managers based their visceral answer solely on anecdotal evidence. Their story began with psychological accounts of Algonquin's management. Many of Algonquin's senior executives had military combat backgrounds. Customers told Freshwater that

Algonquin's sales force was stubborn and unyielding; their representatives would supposedly do just about anything to gain an account. Because of this evidence, Freshwater interpreted a recent Algonquin press release as a clear act of war. Algonquin had publicly announced plans to bring two large production facilities online within the next three years. One of them would help the company achieve a much better cost position, almost on par with Freshwater's own.

When we asked several of Freshwater's managers to pick a customer segment and walk us through the history of each account, the pounding on the war drums stopped and the truth began to emerge. Five large multinational customers composed this segment. Freshwater had an entrenched position at two of them, and earned profits it described as "acceptable to quite high." Algonquin "owned" a third customer. Recent activity at the remaining two customers, though, had fueled Freshwater management's appetite for action. Freshwater had lost one account to Algonquin entirely, and had just lost 10 percent of its volume to Algonquin at the other.

As we explored in detail how Freshwater had lost this business, the managers began to realize that they could not blame their market share losses on the alleged aggressiveness from Algonquin. The customer that Algonquin acquired completely not only had the smallest volume of the five in the segment, it had also suffered for two years under Freshwater's poor service quality and missed delivery deadlines. Algonquin's move to claim the customer arose from opportunity, not any inherent combativeness. It could provide better products and service, and therefore "deserved" the market share.

In the second case, the customer itself had actually approached Freshwater with news that it wanted to expand and secure its supplier base by vetting at least one other vendor for all essential supplies. How could it vet Algonquin without providing it with a real piece of business? If Freshwater were to lose any additional market share at this customer, price would be only one reason among many. Instead, Freshwater needed to take up the challenge and figure out how to provide superior value to this customer than Algonquin could, not lower prices. The focus of our discussion shifted from the original issue listed earlier in the title of this case study to more peaceful questions: How could Freshwater differentiate itself from Algonquin? In particular, how could Freshwater improve its service and logistics? What other advantages could it press in order to outshine Algonquin? To what degree could Freshwater integrate the customer into the development and testing on its next-generation product?

Freshwater's managers admitted that Algonquin had actually stolen nothing from them. In fact, Freshwater *lost* the business more than Algonquin had *won* it. Furthermore, if profits seemed so high at two of Freshwater's main customers, why hadn't Algonquin ever attacked there? Some of the Freshwater managers began to see their "vicious" competitor in a different light that showed it to be quite tame and disciplined. Algonquin started to look like a competitor with superior service, rather than a price-aggressive monster.

Freshwater's management could not adopt a similar philosophy, however, until it learned how to pick its fights. This meant asking the same questions every time it faced the threat of losing business:

- How high is the profit potential in this segment?

- How high is the profit potential at this customer?

- Do we deserve market share because of a strong product advantage, or can we only defend it through lower prices?

- How will our competitor respond if we retaliate?

- How will they respond if we back off?

Each of these questions focuses attention on the quality of revenue at stake, not the amount. One tool that helps managers answer these questions and make informed decisions is the competition map, which we introduce and describe in the next section.

31

Use a Competition Map to Guide Your Decision Making

The market dynamics that Freshwater witnessed raise important strategic questions. If a new company enters your market, do you match it move for move, or do you consciously concede some market share in order to cut your losses and preserve your base of profits? If you take the latter route, where do you make the concessions? If you yourself have achieved a substantial market share through aggressive market entry, do you continue acting aggressively once growth levels off and your product becomes one established product among many others? Or do you become conservative and preserve your profit?

Peaceful competition is the science of profitable differentiation. We say *science* rather than *art* here because picking the right fights and conceding the right market share involves much more than taking a cursory look at basic market data, listening to the war stories your sales force tells, and making some snap judgments about your competitors' next moves.

The mental investment to pick science over art demands two things. First, you must accept the idea that a company can have too much market share, and that gaining more market share than your products warrant—because of the customers' perceived value and your resources to deliver that value—can actually reduce your profits significantly. Second, you must have a full view of your competitive landscape in order to decide where you have the greatest advantages, and what the key points of differentiation are that allow you to pick the areas where to fight for or defend market share and where *not* to fight. We call this view of the landscape a *competition map*.

If Freshwater had used such a map, it would have known immediately that it should not retaliate against Algonquin, because Algonquin held an advantage owing to value that customers recognized and rewarded. Retaliating with lower prices may have lured some of the share back, but with permanent negative ramifications for profit.

32

We'll first explore the issue of how much market share your products warrant. Richard Harmer and Leslie L. Simmel describe this phenomenon in their working paper "How Much Market Share Is Too Much?" According to their theory, a particular product or service reaches the natural limits of its market share when it adds only marginal additional value for the customer. Beyond that point, price becomes the primary differentiator.[3]

To illustrate their point, Harmer and Simmel describe the consequences of the price war that Dell Computer launched in 2001. Before Dell finally backed off, it had raised its share of the personal computer market from 10 percent to 14 percent, an impressive gain. But Harmer and Simmel described the resulting PC market as a "profits wasteland" and estimated that the price war may have cost Dell as much as $2 billion in sacrificed profits.[4]

The theory of Harmer and Simmel does not contradict the PIMS findings we described in the previous chapter. Rather, it shows that the pursuit of market share growth has its limits. Any market share beyond that may not only be undeserved, it could also put future profits at risk.

This leads us to the competition map. The goal of the map is to show where each competitor in the market—in your team's own honest opinion—has a comparative advantage. In other words, it shows where every competitor in the market deserves to be strongest, because of the value it delivers to customers. We refer to those areas as a company's *natural spaces*. This value could derive from superiority in product quality, service, support, delivery capabilities, or any number of other industry-specific requirements. Constructing such a map is possible even in complex markets, in which competitors sell several kinds of products to a diverse range of customers. It requires only three steps.

The easiest step is to create a matrix, as shown in figure 2-2, which has the products on one axis and either customer segments or end-use applications on the other. For purely illustrative purposes,

FIGURE 2-2

The first step in constructing a competition map

	Customer segments		
Products	Blue-collar	White-collar	Students
Doughnuts			
Coffee			
Espresso drinks			
Bagels/cold sandwiches			
Hot breakfast sandwiches			
Lunch sandwiches			
Pastry/cookies			
Tea			

Source: Simon-Kucher & Partners

the authors base the map in figures 2-2 and 2-3 on their own quick-and-dirty assessment of the market for breakfast or lunch on the go in the Boston area. In that market, a large, locally based chain and an upscale coffee house compete for customers in three large segments (blue-collar, white-collar, and student).

The second step in building a competition map is to determine how attractive each cell in this matrix is for your own company. We have found that the most straightforward way to do this is to have a small group of your internal product and marketing experts rate each cell separately according to its size, growth potential, profitability, competitive intensity, and potential for differentiation. Have the experts rate each criterion on a scoring scale (say, a rating scale from 1 to 5), then combine the results into an overall score.

The third step requires you to match each of your competitors to the cells, according to where those competitors would have the best

FIGURE 2-3

A sample competition map for breakfast and lunch in Boston

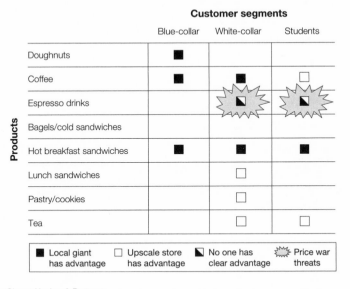

	Customer segments		
	Blue-collar	White-collar	Students
Doughnuts	■		
Coffee	■	■	☐
Espresso drinks		◪	◪
Bagels/cold sandwiches			
Hot breakfast sandwiches	■	■	■
Lunch sandwiches		☐	
Pastry/cookies		☐	
Tea		☐	☐

■ Local giant has advantage   ☐ Upscale store has advantage   ◪ No one has clear advantage   ✴ Price war threats

Source: Simon-Kucher & Partners

chance to capture incremental profit by meeting customer needs through acceptable or superior performance. Only one competitor can occupy an individual cell. We suggest that you use the concept of comparative advantage rather than competitive advantage to assign the competitors to the cells. Using comparative advantage means that you slot some competitors into areas where they put their own resources to best use and provide an acceptable or perhaps superior level of quality to customers, even if they may not currently be best in class.

To understand the difference between competitive advantage and comparative advantage, think of an executive and an administrative assistant. Tasks in an office range from the negotiation of contracts to the management of appointments. Who should take care of what task? To figure that out, you should not look at who does the best job on each task and assign the task accordingly. That would mean you assign jobs according to competitive advantage. Instead, you should assign the tasks so that the executive and the administrative assistant use their skills and talents in such a way that the office runs as efficiently as possible. When you do this, you recognize who has the comparative advantage. Given the time, the executive may be much better at managing his or her calendar—appointments, travel, and other commitments—than the assistant could. He or she would have a competitive advantage over the assistant. But the assistant has the comparative advantage, because the executive's time is better devoted to other tasks.

If you use competitive advantage, you might find that one single supplier would have superior performance in every cell. But that superior supplier cannot achieve that position in every cell and still expect to sustain its level of profit. Left with no other option, rivals would attack it with lower prices in a desperate attempt to defend their own positions or gain new ones. This would plant the seeds for a price war, with the inevitable drain on profits. That is why we suggest using comparative advantage.

To make these assignments of your competitors, you need to make your best assessment of what each one seeks in the market. Ask yourself questions such as:

- What does customer behavior tell us about how well competitors perform?

- What public statements have your competitors made recently regarding their future strategy?

- What resources do your competitors have (value proposition, financial backing, adequate capacity, superior cost position, sales force) to follow through on their goals?

- Has one of your competitors just brought a new plant online or opened a new facility whose output would allow it to serve certain customers?

The finished product would look something like the map in figure 2-3. In this case, the local giant has three clear advantages among blue-collar workers, and also has a clear advantage in hot breakfast sandwiches in all segments. The upscale store, in contrast, has advantages in products (pastry and tea, for example) that appeal to a more white-collar crowd. The strength of each competitor is clear in all of those areas.

The battleground is espresso drinks, which have little relevance for the blue-collar crowd, but a strong appeal among white-collar workers and students. No side has a clear advantage anymore, which creates the risk that one side may try to use price as a differentiating factor. That explains the flash point in those two cells.

Finding other forms of differentiation besides price will, over time, reduce the threat of a price war or even eliminate it entirely. The incumbent (in this case, the upscale store) may need to live with some customer defections in order to preserve its profits.

You can use such a map as a guide to how you should behave in your marketplace. If you are a smaller player, you need to commit your resources to your areas of comparative advantage and make this commitment unequivocally clear to your customers. If you enter other areas of the map, you should proceed as Algonquin did in the Freshwater case earlier. Algonquin did not force its way into Freshwater's customers aggressively. Customers practically invited Algonquin to be their supplier because of their dissatisfaction with Freshwater.

Look selectively for opportunities where customers have received poor service from a competitor, but don't launch an all-out assault on the company in the cell. You could only "win" such an assault through lower prices, and that move is likely to draw a competitive response in an area where you are most vulnerable. Why take that risk?

The competition map gives everybody in your company a clear picture of where to pick battles. You can train yourself and your organization to base your competitive strategy on the desire to earn a high and sustainable profit in a particular part of your market, not on a desire to steal back every lost customer or gain retribution at every turn. Support your commitment through consistent communication to the marketplace. Chapter 10 explains in detail how to do this without risking a violation of antitrust laws. When you have residual positions in areas where another competitor has the comparative advantage, you do not need to defend them aggressively if threatened. In fact, your wisest move may be to cede that market share position to the competitor.

Concede Market Share If It Will Protect Your Profit

When a competitor threatens your position by offering lower prices or by offering a slightly better product at the same price as yours, and you feel that attempt to gain market share is unwarranted, you need to respond quickly and resolutely. Restraint is a viable option, and often the wisest. Control your aggression by suppressing the urge to hit back every single time you lose a piece of business.

You will face a dilemma in the truest sense of the word. You need to choose between two seemingly unattractive alternatives: attack by cutting prices and risking a price war, or defend yourself by stressing the value you provide, at the risk of losing market share to a competitor with lower prices. The latter option, which we usually recommend, demands that you find a true point of differentiation.

For a manufactured product, this point of differentiation often involves services, personal relationships, or simply the ability to deliver a product on time and with consistent quality. But differentiation attempts can also backfire when they are not grounded in something meaningful to the customer, or when your advantage is so slight that customers do not perceive it. When you artificially tweak some feature to make it seem different, most customers see through the gimmick quickly. You end up right where you started.

Many managers remain skeptical when we suggest that they control their aggression when other companies storm their customers. They legitimately ask for a concrete example of a company that did not retaliate and lived to tell about it. We will provide two examples, one from public information and one from our project experience.

CASE STUDY

Issue: How to Respond to a Competitive Threat

Company: Reuters
Product: Financial news and data
Source: Analysis of publicly available information

Thomson Financial undercut the news service giant Reuters on a $1 billion, five-year contract to supply Merrill Lynch with financial news and data at twenty-five thousand terminals. Reuters withdrew instead of trying to match Thomson and hold the business. We would consider the decision tough to swallow, but courageous and correct.

Had Reuters retaliated, it may very well have launched a price war. Thomson may have pressed further, and existing Reuters clients may have seized an opportunity to extract concessions. We refer to this as the *contamination effect* of a successful deal. Rather than set off this landslide and put the industry's profit at risk, Reuters backed off.[5]

The Reuters case is not entirely a matter of high price versus low price. Competitors content with lower profits had already begun to turn the once mighty Reuters' products into commodities. As the advantages of a product diminish, managers tend to lose focus on the nature of the business and the products. Price becomes a tempting means for differentiation. But a price cut by Reuters would have sent an inadvertent signal to its customers. They might have viewed an aggressive response by Reuters, the incumbent, as a defensive maneuver that would implicitly acknowledge that Thomson is a strong competitor from a product value perspective.[6] By conceding the contract to Thomson, Reuters sent a clear message to customers that the market for information services still has a high end and a low one, with Reuters positioned squarely in the former. Implicit in Reuters' response is the belief that its market still has a segment of customers with a high willingness to pay for something more than bits and bytes on a computer screen. They still valued aspects represented by the Reuters brand, like the quality of the information delivered, the length of the relationship, or the nature of the established relationship. Such factors often make companies quite reluctant to switch suppliers just because one supplier offers a lower price.

Had Reuters slashed its prices to keep the Merrill Lynch business, it would have been tantamount to issuing the following communiqué to its remaining customers in that premium segment: "Yes, you are willing to pay more, but please keep your money. We don't want it. Our service is worth less, as we just showed to the folks at Merrill Lynch. So the next time we negotiate with you, feel free to cite that Merrill Lynch deal and use it as the basis for negotiations."

Price contamination occurs when one price concession prompts other customers to ask for similar concessions when they sit down at the negotiating table. Reuters resisted the temptation to contaminate its own prices. It did so in order to preserve its other advantages—no matter how slight they may have become—and it did not need to wait long for the reward. In the eight months after the decision to back off the Merrill Lynch bid, Reuters saw its stock price rise steadily, and its operating profit nearly doubled.

The actions of a company we'll call Mosella Industries provide another cautionary tale on how to respond properly to a competitive threat.

Issue: How to Fend off a Competitive Threat

Company: Mosella Industries
Product: Specialty ceramics
Source: Simon-Kucher & Partners project

Mosella was the market leader in Europe and the United States.[7] The company's only competition came from a handful of smaller companies that served certain niches but could not rival Mosella's product breadth and depth. This situation helped keep price-based competition to a minimum.

The situation took a radical turn, however, when the largest Japanese manufacturer, Nikkoceram, entered the U.S. market. Nikkoceram had substantial financial resources because it had the Japanese market more or less to itself and could charge high prices there.

Mosella assumed that Nikkoceram would enter the U.S. market with extremely aggressive prices, in order to gain a strong market position. Should this happen, Mosella would commit itself to defending its very strong market positions aggressively. The nightmare scenario came true when Nikkoceram launched products at $75 per batch, or 25 percent below Mosella's price of $100 per batch. Customers remained wary of the newcomer, though, and did not stampede to Nikkoceram's siren call. Nonetheless, Mosella sensed a threat. It quickly struck back by slashing its own prices by 20 percent to $80. Mosella's management figured that the slight premium over Nikkoceram would ensure that hardly any customers would switch to the Japanese competitor.

Believing its market share goal was now at risk, Nikkoceram stopped trying to balance market share and profitability and re-directed its energies toward the former. It cut prices by 20 percent to $60, thereby restoring the original 25 percent discount from Mosella's prices. Following this move, customers began to switch for good. As you would expect, Mosella tried to counter by cutting prices once again. Costs prevented Mosella from going below $75, but that made little difference. The battle ended when Nikkoceram had taken a market share of 30 percent. This became the new balance of power in the market.

Mosella's price decreases had compounded the loss of market share. Before Nikkoceram attacked, Mosella charged $100 per batch, which meant it collected $10,000 for every one hundred batches it sold. At the new balance of power, its price had fallen to $75, and it now sold only seventy batches where it used to sell one hundred. That left the company with $5,250 for every $10,000 in revenue it used to generate, a decline of 47.5 percent.

After its attack of the U.S. market, Nikkoceram soon set its sights on Europe, Mosella's home market. Mosella expected the Japanese to attack the same way, but prepared itself differently this time. It had learned its lesson. When the same situation developed again, its management would have a firm idea about how Nikkoceram would respond.

Mosella had to decide between losing around 30 percent of its revenue or almost 50 percent of its revenue. That's certainly not an enviable position, because it appears that you "lose" both ways. Battered and bruised once, Mosella knew it could not "win" this fight. The old approach of protecting every point of market share had cost it dearly. Behaving aggressively once again would exact too great a price. In Europe, it would concede intelligently, and emphasize what makes it different instead of trying to focus entirely on price.

It takes a strong level of business maturity to make any decision that will cost you 30 percent of your revenue. Whether they admit it or not, most managers still want to experience the thrill of winning when faced with that outcome. They would see anything else as a blow to their image. Yet no amount of optimism, confidence, and can-do attitude can overcome the simple math of this situation: you stand to lose 30 percent or 50 percent of your revenue in that market. How can you justify losing 50 percent when you know that you could have contained the damage?

The new approach worked. Mosella kept nearly all prices stable after Nikkoceram came in, as anticipated, with a 25 percent discount to Mosella's prices. Mosella made only slight corrections to maintain certain pieces of business, and saw its weighted average prices fall by only four percent. Nikkoceram eventually gained 30 percent of the market, but market prices had remained at much higher levels.

Mosella could not help but be satisfied with its decision to restrain itself. Although it lost 30 percent of its volume, it shed only 4 percent on price. For every $10,000 it formerly sold in Europe, it now sold $6,720, or 32.8 percent less. Although that seems like defeat, the performance is still almost 15 percentage points better than the disastrous decline of 47.5 percent it experienced in the U.S. market. The restraint—and the higher price levels that resulted from it—had helped Mosella preserve its profits.

The fact that Nikkoceram did not achieve more than 30 percent market share, despite the low prices, shows once again that even in mature markets with similar or fungible products, aspects such as brand, relationship, and switching costs can play an important role in a customer's willingness to pay. Mosella realized this the second time around.

Summary

Many competitors in mature markets destroy profit through aggressive or acquiescent behavior. They try to increase their market share through lower prices without regard for the profit implications. They often use military terminology to describe competition and justify their behavior. Peaceful competitors base their behavior on profit, restraint, and differentiation. They cede market share when they come under attack and realize that they cannot defend that market share profitably. They also differentiate themselves on subtle but important factors (service, support, relationships, brand) rather than through lower prices.

As the Freshwater case showed, an aggressive attitude can blind a company to the real reasons why customers switch suppliers and how a supplier can win them back. To pick their fights intelligently, managers can rely on tools such as a competition map. These maps tell them where they have a comparative advantage, where they should defend share, and where mounting a defense could contaminate their ability to earn profits.

Peaceful competitors also make sure they know the profit implications of every move they make in the market. The cases of Reuters and Mosella clearly show that having such knowledge can prevent costly strategic mistakes. The next chapter explores how you can avoid those mistakes yourself by challenging your assumptions and "doing the math."

CHAPTER 3

Change the Way You
Form Your Assumptions

If we want to move forward, we have to challenge the conventional
wisdom. And that means being very direct. Sometimes you
have to kick people right in their certainties.

—Pascal Brosset, vice president
for innovation and strategy, SAP[1]

CHALLENGING and changing your existing assumptions about your customers is the most important first step in identifying your hidden profit opportunities. It is always easier to retool your thinking—your assumptions about what your customers want and what they're willing to pay—than to retool the actual products and services you offer.

Even in the medium term, you have limited opportunity to make meaningful physical changes to your established products. But you can change the way you do business with your customers. Challenging your assumptions means asking yourself those questions you think you answered definitively years ago. And it means answering these questions not with your reflexes, but with facts and fresh insights drawn from the market.

Base Views of Customers on Facts,
Not Conventional Wisdom

As odd as it may sound, managers make decisions every day that are not based on objective evidence. Instead, they depend heavily on assumptions drawn from the company's collective history or from the industry as a whole. Such *conventional wisdom* is any idea, notion, or rule of thumb that managers apply reflexively and without question. People settle into a particular view of the way their world works; conventional wisdom provides managers with day-to-day guidance. It derives from a natural human tendency to rely on experience rather than the facts at hand when making decisions.

A study published in *Nature* describes how individuals use current information and past experiences to make decisions, a mental process known as Bayesian analysis.[2] When the level of uncertainty spikes—as it would, say, if a manager heard news about an intensifying competitive threat at a key account—it can cause a person to rely more heavily on past experience than on the actual facts. Most people, then, opt for a preprogrammed response fueled by anecdotal evidence. Conventional wisdom can often triumph over objectivity whenever anecdotal evidence seems overwhelmingly convincing.

Think back to the last time you purchased a car. You may have downloaded a wide range of data to help you make your decision. You looked at detailed ratings from objective consumer watchdogs, perused surveys on customer satisfaction, and studied data on safety and performance. Let's assume you have finally settled on the make and model of car you want to purchase.

The night before you plan to go the dealership, you attend a party. The discussion turns to cars, and you reveal your purchase decision. Then a guest relates his own experience with the car you've just decided to buy. In rather colorful and blunt language, he describes the car as unreliable and uncomfortable and says the dealer's service has disappointed him time and again. He strongly recommends that you reconsider your choice.

If you react as most people do, you probably reconsider. But step back for a moment and think that decision through. This party guest's opinion constitutes a sample of one. In contrast, all those ratings and surveys you've already read derive their results and conclusions from tens of thousands of that car's owners, all with individual opinions both glowing and glaring.

The database for your car decision grew from 50,000 to 50,001 after your encounter with the party guest. If you reconsidered, you gave that party guest's opinion more weight than you gave the opinions of 50,000 other people. Just who was this party guest anyway?

Sadly, managers behave much the same way whenever they latch onto the most recent set of facts that impressed them, and extrapolate from there. They generalize from single observations, even if the data from thousands of other observations tells them they shouldn't. We call this the curse of anecdotal evidence.

Management consultant Charles Roxburgh argues that one shouldn't categorically criticize people who make their decisions that way. To some degree it is nature's fault, not theirs. Managers struggle to break away from an intuitive decision process that is hardwired into our brains. In his article "Hidden Flaws in Strategy," Roxburgh cites the "false consensus effect," a natural tendency for people to recall only those experiences that reinforce their own assumptions or help them to find counterexamples to contradict any kind of rigorous evaluation.[3] Regardless of how many files their organization collects or how many Excel spreadsheets clog their teams' hard drives, managers' decision making derives from a small, selective store of information they continue to accumulate in the same way from the same sources until it lets them down. It becomes their information habit and can prevent them from seeing the obvious, because no one checks or validates old assumptions anymore.

Left unchecked, the resulting conventional wisdom can work as an insidious poison. When managers ignore the facts at hand for the sake of past experience, they increase the chances that they will continue to overlook additional profit opportunities. Conventional wisdom blinds an organization both to its customers' true preferences and to the profit opportunities those preferences create. Companies used to make finer distinctions among customers, but these have dulled over time. Managers refuse to sharpen those distinctions again because it would mean going against "the way we do business around here." The following case underscores this point.

CASE STUDY

Issue: Challenging Existing Assumptions About Customers

Company: Dakota Devices
Product: Testing device
Source: Simon-Kucher & Partners project

Dakota, a large diversified industrial supplier, manufactures both analog and digital devices for testing whether certain kinds of production machinery comply with government regulations.[4] Plant managers or operators must conduct the test once per day, usually before the first morning shift.

Long a market leader in selling the analog versions, Dakota nonetheless struggled to make inroads with the digital version, which it had priced at a premium of 15 percent above the analog device. The sluggish sales growth frustrated the product's marketing team. As we analyzed this issue, members of the team elaborated on the options they had considered thus far. They wondered whether they should lower their prices, offer other incentives to encourage customers to convert, or alter the product to make it more appealing.

Before exploring which alternative might bring the highest profit, we wanted to understand more about the benefits the product offered and why they mattered. "Why exactly would these people switch from analog to digital and pay a 15 percent premium for your product?" we asked. The marketing team, which included many of the engineers and chemists who helped develop the device, looked at each other as if they might find the right answer written on one of their colleagues' foreheads. Then the lead scientist placed the product on the table, looked our team in the eyes, and spoke with all the restraint he could muster.

"This," he said, "is protected by seven patents."

The argument made perfect sense to the engineers, who took considerable pride in such accomplishments. They even received monetary incentives to file patents. Their ingrained rule of thumb told them that the more patents a product has, the better it must be. They took for granted the conclusion that customers would use the same rule of thumb and decide that a product with many patents must deliver superior performance.

The team, though, demonstrated less confidence in its answers to our remaining questions. They were uncertain whether the device did anything that went unnoticed by customers, because they viewed it as a straightforward—albeit a technologically superior—testing device. Asked whether some customer groups may be getting too good a deal, they said that a compliance test is a compliance test. That's a pretty straightforward "deal," so it would be hard to make it "too good." And how would competitors argue against them, we asked? "Price," they said in unison.

Their view of the market seemed oversimplified. Deciding that there may be a better way to answer the questions, the team agreed to interview a small sample of current and potential customers. By focusing on the customers' preferences and willingness to pay, Dakota employed the same type of research we will explain in greater detail in chapter 5. The team members showed a willingness to test their assumptions and, more importantly, to accept the results and use them as the basis for their marketing decisions.

The results surprised the marketing team. Customers were either too jaded or too sophisticated to be convinced by talk of how many patents the product had. Most could not have cared less. But their responses revealed some sharp differences in how they planned to use the digital device. Whereas some customers confirmed Dakota's internal view (that "a test is just a test"), others wanted to use the device several times a day, not just before the first shift. Many factors could affect machine performance, from energy consumption to internal temperature and pressure to cycle time. By tracking each aspect of machine performance throughout the day, customers could diagnose potential problems and perform preventive maintenance. This use created a substantial business benefit for the customer, because it would help plants increase productivity and reduce maintenance costs. Most indicated they would pay a premium price for something that allowed them to cut energy costs, reduce the number of emergency maintenance calls, and avoid surprise production shutdowns. These facts and insights made it clear to team members that they would have additional profit opportunities to capitalize on if they changed their assumptions about their customers. Changing the product itself was unnecessary.

Don't Let Customers Take You for Granted

Industrial companies whose products have a high degree of standardization often underestimate the importance of what benefits they deliver beyond the product. In contrast, managers who achieve superior profit performance in a mature market appreciate that service, logistics, technical support, and marketing support can form the basis of meaningful differentiation. It's where profit opportunities reside. Even good rapport with a customer has a monetary value when it discourages a customer from switching suppliers.

A service offering can range from online self-serve technical help to a comprehensive program involving support such as consulting, engineering, inventory management, and customized shipping. In such markets, the breadth and quality of these service offerings can form a critical point of differentiation. But how do companies determine which customer receives what services and how much the customer should pay for them? Many industrial firms, unfortunately, do not make such determinations and distinctions. At a conference, one of the authors had the following conversation with a senior manager of a *Fortune* 500 company whose physical products differ little from those of its competitors:

"Do you charge for next-day delivery?"
"No."
"Do you charge for odd lots?"
"No."
"Do you charge for nonstandard sizes or lengths?"
"No. That's all included. We just charge by the square foot."

This senior manager is not alone. A manager from a global industrial conglomerate described in greater detail how his company's pricing structure has not evolved over time, even though customer requirements and his company's products and services have.

"In the past we just sold product, but now I would estimate that consulting and testing makes up at least 80 percent of the value we deliver," he said. The product itself is considered to be "a minor part of the whole equation." You won't, however, find the price list for these consulting and testing services. It doesn't exist. The company charges its clients for all value delivered in exactly the same way it has done for decades: based strictly on the pounds of product purchased.

Think about these descriptions for a moment. If all of these services are included in the overall price, then these companies sell service by the square foot or service by the pound. In such situations, we feel it is legitimate to ask how much a pound of service should cost. And how does it convert into a square foot of service?

The questions sound odd, but most manufacturers of industrial products grapple with such questions every day, even though few frame them in those terms. Ask their sales or marketing managers how much their companies charge for service, and you will receive an abrupt answer along the lines of "You can't charge for service in our industry" or "It's included because our customers expect it." In a culture of acquiescence, managers take these assumptions for granted. A few cling to them ferociously, as if the very idea of asking customers to pay for services would embarrass them and expose them as someone who "just doesn't get it."

The case of Peninsula Auto Alloys shows how a company can change its viewpoint on service when it makes a commitment to introspection and remains open to alternative ideas.[5] This new thought process helped Peninsula become aware of the profit buried within its service programs, which it had traditionally treated as deal sweeteners rather than the basis for a meaningful and valuable competitive advantage.

CASE STUDY

Issue: Understand the Importance
Customers Place on Service

Company: Peninsula Auto Alloys
Product: Alloys in cars
Source: Simon-Kucher & Partners project

The team members responsible for one "semicommodity" product at Peninsula had no difficulty believing that they had some

additional profit opportunities they had not yet identified or captured. It offered them hope at a time when pressure from purchasing
departments at original equipment manufacturers (OEMs) had become immense. They could not pin their hopes on a breakthrough.
The technology behind the actual product this team sold day to day
was more than a half century old. Some of the technologies it competed against were even older. A new or modified product was entirely out of the question.

Senior managers had strong feelings that this business unit overlooked profit nearly every time its salespeople negotiated a contract.
If some customers paid significantly more for the same amount of
physical product, because of differences in service levels, why could-
n't they get the others to do so? What do they have to do to get that
money in the future?

During our first briefing, the sales director grinned when we
broached the question of charging for service.

"We can't do that," she said.

We challenged that hypothesis by taking a closer look at what her
sales team actually *did* in each deal, not just what they sold. Examining
what the sales team did in each deal required a painstaking and honest
reconstruction of real-life negotiations from beginning to end. It involved more than just taking notes as the team told its war stories. The
team members took us step-by-step through a handful of deals, from
the initial contact or request for proposal (RFP) to the awarding of
the contract, including the relevant trail of faxes, letters, and e-mails.
We will describe this process in more detail in chapters 4 and 5.

Together with their sales team, we learned that deals seemed to
go off or stay on course for the same respective reasons. Many of the
differences between deals arose from how the sales representatives
treated service. A few salespeople considered service as something
that added a legitimate value for which the customer should pay a
premium. But most salespeople used it as a bargaining chip without
taking either willingness to pay or internal costs into account.

This work yielded consensus on four hypotheses regarding Peninsula's interactions with its customers. Two explained why the team did well, the remaining two where or why it fell short. According to these hypotheses, Peninsula felt confident that it

- *Knew how customers make buying decisions.* The purchaser has the strongest influence.

- *Knew the market prices well.* The team felt it had a good feeling for when its prices matched customers' willingness to pay.

- *Was "stuck in the middle" of the market.* In most negotiations, the team felt customers with a strong quality orientation would go with one of Peninsula's nationally known competitors, while strongly "cost oriented" ones would opt for a smaller domestic or foreign supplier. This left Peninsula sandwiched in between.

- *Undersold itself.* The team felt it entered negotiations with a chip on its shoulder and did not take advantage of its strengths.

To confirm or refute these hypotheses, the sales director commissioned a dozen interviews with her largest customers and with a couple of smaller ones that they thought would emerge as major customers over the next five years. The key challenge was to conduct this small-scale but in-depth research anonymously and to avoid direct questions regarding specific price levels or comparisons of specific competitors.

In this case, the customers confirmed only one of the four hypotheses: Peninsula had indeed sold itself short during negotiations. As for the remaining three, the customers called one into question and refuted two of them outright. Peninsula was not stuck in the middle in the minds of the customers. Instead, it ranked as the preferred supplier for some customers and a viable alternative for others. The assumption that foreign or "low cost" competitors posed a threat proved unfounded. The foreign competitors had little visibility for the customers. Some customers had never even met a foreign sales representative, while other customers questioned the commitment that low-cost suppliers would have to service and support.

What made the difference for Peninsula? Customers cited Peninsula's exceptional level of personalized service, an area whose importance and value Peninsula had continually underestimated. It had a unique combination of on-site presence, development capabilities, and a down-to-earth willingness to pitch in when a crisis or bottleneck emerged. This served as a clear switching barrier and formed its strongest line of defense against most low-cost competitors, especially the foreign competitors that lacked resources to provide the same level of on-site service.

Peninsula believed that customers took the company and its services for granted. In reality, product quality is what customers took for granted. No customer even remotely considered it a point of differentiation. Ironically, service is the area where companies like Peninsula cut back in order to save costs. It is dangerous to assume that the most costly and resource-draining investments you make—such as working overtime with customers on-site at their own facilities—are the areas where you overdeliver or where the customer takes you for granted. These could actually be the heart and soul of your company's competitive advantage.

The Peninsula business unit also did not have the strongest grip on either the customer's decision-making process or the prices they expected. A purchaser rarely made the decision on which supplier to use. Most of the partners interviewed said the purchaser had one task: namely, to extract a lower price from the supplier that the design team or engineer had already preselected.

By gaining a better understanding of how customers viewed their services, and how that view differed from customer to customer, Peninsula Auto Alloys stopped trying to be all things to all customers. It replaced the carte blanche approach to service and instead began to make successful moves to charge explicitly for certain services. It also ensured that the prices it negotiated with customers better reflected the whole package the customer actually received.

Take Advantage of the Powerful Link Between Price and Profit

To identify and tap profit opportunities, you need to make improvements in all aspects of your marketing mix. In the short term, however, you achieve the greatest direct impact on profits by optimizing your pricing. This includes your processes for devising price structures and setting the prices themselves. You cannot pursue profit opportunities without a fundamental understanding of the link between price and profit.

Your company makes money only when customers pay you. It makes sense, then, that your profits depend on how well you price your products. If you plot your profit against the prices you could conceivably charge for your product, what would that kind of curve look like? In most cases, it would have a shape similar to the curve in figure 3-1, which we derived from one of our clients' actual data and estimates.

A plot of profit versus price will always have a maximum point, an identifiable summit. The goal of managers of mature products in mature markets should be to find that summit for their products and services, and focus their marketing on getting the company as close as possible to the peak profit dollars that summit represents.

If your prices are too low, you sacrifice profits because the increased volume you sell does not compensate for your lower margin per unit. You also sacrifice profits if your prices are too high,

FIGURE 3-1

How close are you to the price point that maximizes your profit?

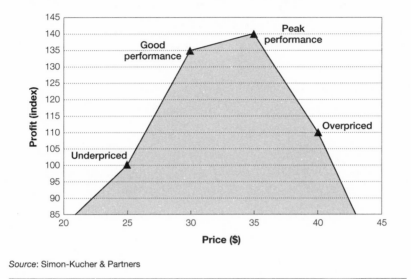

Source: Simon-Kucher & Partners

because the higher margins per unit do not offset the lower volumes. We will refer to figure 3-1 frequently throughout the book to reinforce how important it is for you to understand these relationships. It demonstrates that when you try to find the optimal trade-off between volume and price, there is always a right equation that brings the greatest profit. Unless you know what your own profit curve looks like, you won't know where your "right answer" is, nor will you know how much money this missing piece of information costs you every time you make a sale.

Take a price of $25 per unit in figure 3-1. Charging this price per unit would earn you a profit level of 100 on an indexed basis. This index does not represent a profit margin or some other measure of profitability. It represents absolute dollars. Imagine sacks of money you get to keep and store in your safe. The higher the index, the more sacks you can stash away. We have named this point "underpriced" because the company would have a considerable profit upside if it raised prices.

Were you to charge $30 per unit, you would obviously sell fewer units, but your profit index would rise to 135 from 100, an increase of 35 percent. This point bears the name "good performance."

The ascent from "underpriced" to "good performance" also reveals a dynamic that causes controversy in nearly every company the authors have ever encountered: the tension between market share and profit. As we explained in the introductory chapter, market share and profit represent incompatible goals in highly contested, mature markets unless you have a breakthrough innovation or an unassailable cost advantage. This cultural conflict pits managers who favor aggression and acquiescence against those who favor profit, restraint, and differentiation. As we progress through this book, we will continue to build the case that the latter group of managers should prevail in this conflict.

The curve in figure 3-1 peaks at a price of $35 per unit, which raises the profit index to 140. Any price above or below $35 will reduce your profit. Raise prices to $40 per unit, and your profit index drops from 140 to 110, a decline of 21 percent. We have named this fourth point "overpriced."

For every product and service you have, you can determine where your point of "peak performance," the summit on the curve, actually lies along the profit curve. Likewise, you can determine when you have significantly underpriced or overpriced your products. In chapters 4 and 5, we will show you how you can draw these curves for your own products, using either internal or external data. Your profit curves may be flatter or steeper than the one shown in figure 3-1. Right now, though, we will describe the important role they should play in setting prices in your organization.

"Good performance" represents by far the most interesting area. In our project work, we rarely see extreme situations in which a company's current pricing would place it below the "underpriced" level or beyond "overpriced." Most companies we work with have managed to climb to within striking distance of "good performance." They're good at what they do. But they may not have sighted "peak performance" yet.

In other words, they know neither how profitable they ought to be, nor that that optimal level of profit is definable and achievable. This statement would be little more than an esoteric ivory-tower abstraction were one simple fact not true: managers can succeed in identifying and capturing the difference between "good performance" and "peak performance" for their company's products and services. When they do, the increased annual profit usually amounts to millions of dollars and far exceeds the investment required.

In figure 3-1 the move from "good" to "peak" raises the profit index just 5 points, from 135 to 140. That may seem like a minor difference, but it will still increase your profits by 3.7 percent. For a company with $1 billion in revenue and $100 million in operating profit, it means an extra $3.7 million per year in additional profit. Every product or service has a price at which it achieves peak profit performance. If your prices put you left or right of that peak, you have not priced your products and services for profit. You have left money in your customers' pockets.

How can you reach this profit summit? You must see it first. If you rely entirely on your gut feeling and conventional wisdom—as reflected in shortcuts such as cost-plus pricing—finding the summit would be pure coincidence. In the meantime, the further you fall short of the summit, the more profit you are surrendering.

Oddly, conventional wisdom on pricing ignores the link we just described between pricing and profit. Conventional wisdom for setting prices provides you with two options: the cost-plus method (which means price is some multiple of your costs) and the "look at the competition" method (which means price is some multiple of what your competitors charge). In one survey, Wied-Nebbeling found that about 70 percent of firms apply some version of cost-plus pricing.[6] Since the mid-1990s Simon-Kucher & Partners has periodically surveyed senior and C-level executives at large global companies on their pricing strategies and techniques. One set of questions focuses on the types of information they use to make pricing decisions and how well informed they feel. Some 81 percent of the respondents in one survey considered themselves well informed about variable costs, and 75 percent felt well informed about where competitors' prices stood. But only 34 percent felt comfortable with their knowledge of *price response*, the key to drawing the profit curves. Price response represents the shift in demand when you increase or decrease your price. Closely related to it is the concept of *price elasticity*, which represents the percentage change in customer demand, divided by the percentage change in price. If you cut your prices by 10 percent and your unit sales rise by 10 percent, your price elasticity would be one. Your revenue stays roughly the same, but your profit drops, because you have to sell more units to earn that same revenue.

Why does the very lucrative concept of a profit curve and the knowledge that you really can figure out where your most profitable price point is fail to resonate with more managers? Perhaps the most important reason is that managers feel they have no practical alternative to replace their established and convenient methods, cost-plus and look-at-the-competition.

Like all conventional wisdom, cost-plus and look-at-the-competition have certain advantages. It is no surprise, then, that most managers use what they know best, what they can easily observe and count, as their basis for price setting. The methods have a quantitative character and a logical foundation. The cost-plus method is also "simple and easy to apply. It is based on hard cost data and seemingly copes with market uncertainty."[7] Finally, managers have learned to live with the drawbacks of these methods.

Pricing literature, in contrast, holds neither of these shortcut methods in high regard. Dolan and Simon, who noted the few advantages just mentioned, quickly point out the flaws: "It is foolish not to explicitly consider the demand side in setting prices. The customer's willingness to pay is not determined by the costs of a product but by its performance and resulting value to its customer."[8] Nagle and Holden refer to the cost-plus method as the "cost plus delusion." They claim that "cost-plus pricing is, historically, the most common pricing procedure because it carries an aura of financial prudence. Financial prudence, according to this view, is achieved by pricing every product or service to yield a fair return over all costs, fully and fairly allocated. In theory, it is a simple guide to profitability; in practice, it is a blueprint for mediocre financial performance."[9]

The pricing that DaimlerChrysler's Chrysler division adopted for its 300 model shows how dramatic the profit sacrifice can be if a company relies on cost-plus to set its prices. Customers could purchase a 300 with a standard V-6 engine or with the 350-horsepower engine based on the Hemi technology the company developed in the 1960s. Both engines cost roughly the same to manufacture. If Chrysler management had used cost-plus pricing, it would have had no reason to charge a premium for the more powerful engine. Instead, "the Hemi version, called the 300C, sells for almost $10,000 more. While that model includes leather seats and other expensive features, analysts believe most of the difference is pure profit."[10] While we have no way to know without further analysis whether Chrysler maximized its profit with a premium of $10,000, the point is clear. Chrysler generates gross revenues of $1 billion for every 100,000 Hemi-powered 300Cs it sells, and much of that revenue ends up as profit.

Beware the Competitive Benchmark!

One problem with basing your prices on your competitors' prices is the relevance of those prices to your business. Price cuts by aggressive, low-end competitors may not have any short-term consequences in terms of market share for your products if you operate at the higher end of the market. Therefore, their price cuts should not draw a response from you. As we demonstrated in chapter 2, responding to price cuts from established competitors can likewise be inadvisable, because it risks a further counterresponse that will trigger a price war.

As you prepare to make a competition map, as outlined in the previous chapter, you will obviously require some level of intelligence about your competitors and make decisions based on that information. But you should make a distinction between addressing fundamental questions about their strengths and weaknesses in order to complete the map, and succumbing to the temptation of letting competitors guide your entire strategy.

It is natural for managers to obsess over what their competitors are doing. They behave like sports fans watching the out-of-town scores as their team fights for a playoff berth or tries to fend off relegation.

Mick Jagger, lead singer and senior partner of the Rolling Stones, once said that if "U2 and Madonna costs $100, you don't want to be charging $200. I try to keep ticket prices within the market range."[11] Our question to Sir Mick is, "Why?" Front-row seats for his band's shows in Boston's Fleet Center arena in 2002 sold on the aftermarket for several hundred dollars, and some radio stations auctioned them for well over $1,000. The willingness to pay for these tickets is huge. Much of the older baby boom audience that attends Stones concerts has the disposable income to afford this kind of special occasion.

The problem is that Sir Mick has focused his attention on the presumed competition rather than on what his own band really deserves. What if Rolling Stones fans don't care about Madonna concert ticket prices, because they would never go anyway? What if Madonna's management made a misjudgment the last time it set prices? Even worse, perhaps it made that misjudgment as a response to something the Stones or Bruce Springsteen or someone else did, which might itself have been a misjudgment.

As soon as one competitor makes a marketing misstep, all those who follow that lead will perpetuate and compound the error until prices no longer bear any relation to what customers are willing to pay. Consider the implications of Sir Mick's comment for your own business.

When you set prices against your competition's, chances are high that your competition sets their prices against yours. Your actions depend on what you feel the competition has done, or may do next, rather than how much your customers are willing to pay. Competitors' prices are without doubt an important driver of your customers' willingness to pay. That's why it is even more important for you not to force your competitors into doing something reckless (hence the competition map). When we hear managers explain how they price against competitors' prices, we immediately ask them how they would react if they knew their chief competitor—at that very same moment—was discussing *its* prices in the same manner.[12]

The moral of this story is that in mature markets, your customers will tell you everything that is relevant about your competition and everything about how you should set up your marketing mix profitably. It is more effective to observe how customers behave than the competitors themselves. While you should not neglect competitive intelligence entirely, you should focus your resources on customer intelligence. Chapters 4 and 5 will show you how you can gather better customer intelligence.

Summary

Managers in mature markets tend to rely on mental shortcuts when they make decisions. They rely on anecdotal evidence and industry conventional wisdom instead of objective evidence and fact-based assumptions. As a result, they underestimate the importance and value of what they do for their customers

Perhaps the biggest and most costly abuse of conventional wisdom is in the area of pricing. Pricing shortcuts include cost-plus pricing and pricing to the competition. Overcoming these and other shortcuts represents a major source of additional profit.

Managers can earn a large amount of additional profit if they do the math to understand how the prices they charge affect the profit they earn. The profit curve (figure 3-1) shows that every product or service has a price at which a company achieves its maximum profit. Any price higher or lower than that optimum will cost you money. There are no exceptions.

If you do not base your prices on a profit curve, the price you pick for your product is at best an educated guess, at worst a mistake that could permanently destroy your company's ability to earn money. The alternative, again, is to remain focused on profit and to base your marketing assumptions and decisions on the most solid evidence possible.

You can begin this process by understanding and analyzing the data you already have. The next chapter points out what you should look for.

CHAPTER 4

Use Internal Data
to Find Profit Opportunities

Math decisions always trump opinion and judgment. The trouble
with most corporations is that they make judgment-based decisions
when data-based decisions could be made.
—Jeff Wilke, head of customer service, Amazon.com[1]

CUSTOMER INTELLIGENCE—about their preferences, about their buying behavior—can help you make a number of decisions based on fact, not conventional wisdom. This chapter will show you how to analyze and interpret data you already have within your company or in your head. You don't automatically need to commission a survey every time you have a question about your customers. While your internal data clearly has limitations, it can tell you a lot about what your customers want, what they do, and how they respond to competitive threats.

Begin by Letting Internal Data
Guide Your Decision Making

John D. C. Little, professor at the MIT Sloan School of Management, differentiates between two types of data: status data and response data.[2] Much of the data companies can retrieve in their own data-bases is *status data*. This includes revenue, unit sales, variable costs, price levels, market share estimates, and the size of advertising budgets. Depending on how transparent the market is, a typical company will even have much of this information about its competitors.

Analyzing status data can reveal areas where you have opportunities to differentiate, redirect your sales and marketing resources, and earn more profit as a result. But the greatest profit gains come from generating what Little termed *response data*. Response data includes price elasticities, advertising effectiveness, and sales effectiveness. This data always involves an independent (causal) variable and a dependent variable, representing the response or effect. Pure comparisons over time, such as your change in market share from year to year, are not response data, because they offer no insight into the "why" question. You can only obtain response data with dynamic comparisons (before and after) of your status data and/or the results of test markets. This data helps give you the most precise indication of where you have opportunities for additional profit.

In the remainder of this chapter, we will show you how to use your internal data to gain insights into your customers, find potential points of differentiation, make changes to your marketing mix, and even quantify the extent of the incremental profit you should pursue. We will focus primarily on customer-related data that already exists within your company.

Use Status Data to Identify Your Profit Opportunities

Why do we make a big deal about these internal data sets? The reason is simple. No matter how profitable a company might be overall, its managers are often unsure about whether the company is as profitable as it could be or should be. To draw that conclusion and earn

FIGURE 4-1

Status and response data most companies have available

What information is available?		How fast?	Who could analyze it?
Status data	Volume, revenue, price, variable cost by ☐ Customer segment? ☑ Product group? ☐ Region? ☑ Sales representative? ☐ _____	☐ Immediately available ☐ <4 weeks ☑ 2–3 months	☑ Financial analyst ☐ Marketing support ☐ _____
Response data	☑ Product change response ☐ Price response ☑ Promotion/advertising response ☐ _____ each – by customer segment – by product group – by region	☐ Requires new software system	

Source: Simon-Kucher & Partners

that extra profit, they need a better understanding of whether the thousands of individual decisions their teams make each year are profit- or loss-making, wise or unwise, essential or unnecessary. In figure 4-1 we take a closer look at the kinds of status and response data companies tend to have available.

You might expect companies, especially large ones with IT departments and customer relations departments, to have a compact, complete set of status data for managers to work with. At an aggregated level, this may be true. But try retrieving data broken down into customer, region, product, or salesperson, and you will quickly find yourself frustrated.

The status data that can help you understand your customers is rarely in an easily and quickly accessible form. Most of our projects begin with helping clients bring the data they do have into a common framework. When the data does exist, we usually find it spread across many departments. In some organizations the people who manage the data in different departments rarely, if ever, talk to each other, and for very good reasons. They have different allegiances, receive pay and resources from different budgets, and have completely different objectives and incentives. As a result, we usually encounter one of the following two roadblocks:

- *The company doesn't have exactly what it needs.* The good news is that the data is usually there . . . sort of. It just does not exist at the level of detail required for relevant analyses. You find aggregates and averages, but no detailed breakdowns according to products, customers, or sales teams. That leaves the door open for subjectivity, intuition, and experience to fill in the gaps that data should fill.

- *The company can get the data, but it will take a while.* It often takes weeks or even months for companies to bring their data together in one place. When we asked a manufacturer of household goods to provide us with data on wholesale and retail prices in five European countries and the United States, its team needed three months to reconcile the data.

Once you have a common framework together, you would benefit from putting a team in place to make sure the data set remains up-to-date and to analyze the data. Even companies with fully deployed enterprise resource planning software packages struggle with this seemingly simple task. This has created a niche for software vendors that consolidate existing data in meaningful and flexible ways.

A company we'll call Northlight Sanitation (Northsan) accomplished the tasks we described earlier and then put that data to use. Although analyses of status data are not as revealing as analyses of response data (which we explain in the next section), Northsan nonetheless used its status data to expose a fresh source of potential profits.

Issue: Understand Revenue and Profit by Salesperson

Company: Northlight Sanitation
Product: Kitchen and bathroom fixtures
Source: Simon-Kucher & Partners project

Northsan manufactures and sells a wide range of fixtures and accessories for kitchens and bathrooms. The company used a simple but effective analysis to find pockets of additional profit within its organization once it found a way to bring its data together in a useful way.[3]

Ranked among the market leaders, Northsan had a large sales force that sold to wholesalers as well as directly to contractors. The company granted the salespeople considerable leeway in negotiating prices, terms, and conditions. Top management felt that this approach helped the company acquire and keep important pieces of business in an increasingly competitive marketplace. Historically, Northsan had only limited capabilities to break down information to the level of the individual salesperson. Beyond comparing revenue, it could not easily compare one salesperson's performance directly with another's. The salespeople could argue—correctly—that the competition, the types of customers, and the product portfolio Northsan makes available all differ from territory to territory. But the company expected these differences to be slight enough that they would not distort the overall picture. It never bothered to dig deeper.

After Northsan consolidated its data into one common framework, it began to examine finer breakdowns. You will find one of the first reports the company generated in figure 4-2, which shows Northsan's usual metric, net sales, for twenty selected salespeople. Now, however, Northsan could also determine the contribution margin each salesperson achieved.

FIGURE 4-2

Performance of salespeople at Northsan

Salesperson	Revenue per salesperson	Contribution margin
A0071	$1,750,127	9.7%
A2723	$1,701,336	5.3%
A3010	$1,452,975	10.0%
A0602	$1,317,975	10.2%
A2761	$1,276,251	6.3%
A0109	$1,274,088	9.6%
A2697	$1,087,099	7.3%
A0107	$1,038,523	9.8%
A1506	$1,002,236	9.5%
A2704	$900,044	5.9%
A0365	$886,176	6.7%
A0323	$870,473	6.0%
A1561	$865,473	7.5%
A1600	$806,065	10.1%
A1725	$785,291	23.0%
A1461	$756,569	9.7%
A1505	$738,686	8.0%
A2767	$727,472	6.4%
A0260	$709,873	10.3%
A1604	$707,009	14.8%

Source: Simon-Kucher & Partners project

Notice that one salesperson (identified as A2704) generates just over $900,000 in sales, but the contribution margin on those sales is 5.9 percent. In contrast, sales by A1725 were only $785,000, but at a much higher contribution margin of 23 percent. Both cases are circled in figure 4-2.

While Northsan already knew the differences in sales performance and the resulting sales commissions it paid, the profit-margin picture caught the company by surprise. Nobody had expected the contribution margins generated by salespeople to vary so widely.

The old arguments about territorial differences and special circumstances could not explain away the fact that the contribution
margins salespeople generated differed by as much as a factor of five.
The new hypothesis was that the sales representatives with the lowest
contribution margins either acted too aggressively in the market or
put up little or no resistance to customer demands.

Rather than interpret the data literally, Northsan decided to
probe further in order to understand why some of the former "star"
performers in the organization (in terms of revenue) did not generate much profit. The company interviewed sales representatives, ac-
companied some of them on sales calls, and held follow-up discussions with selected customers.

The result of extra analysis was startlingly clear. The company
had two types of sales representatives. One type could articulate
Northsan's value proposition well and held its ground when customers sought lower prices. The other group tried to increase sales by
regularly and actively offering lower prices, generous rebates, or encouraging customers to switch to lower-margin products. They sold
as much product as possible, but with a clear disregard for the company's profits.

Northsan took two steps to correct the problem. It retrained, re-
assigned, or terminated the salespeople who chased only volume. It
also adjusted its incentive system to reward contribution more than
unit sales. These two steps boosted Northsan's return on sales from
11.6 percent to almost 14 percent. This improvement is in line with
the amount we mentioned back in chapter 1. We said that companies
have a vast profit potential—equivalent to 1 to 3 percent of their
annual revenue—hidden in their sales and marketing departments.

Without the better view of its status data, Northsan would have
continued to reward the company's volume sellers for destroying
profit. Without stepping back to interpret the new data, it would

have reflexively blamed the offenders without a clearer understanding of the underlying patterns. In this case, the company's incentive system truly had encouraged and reinforced the observed behavior. It is hard to blame a salesperson for achieving the level of performance you paid them to reach. We discuss sales force incentives in greater detail in chapter 9.

Generate Response Data to Quantify Your Profit Opportunities

The success of your product—how much of it you sell—is inseparable from how much you charge (price) and how much you invest (other marketing initiatives). An attempt to establish any kind of sales target, craft a response to a competitive threat, or change your marketing approach makes no sense without having a clear understanding of the impact of price and marketing investment. To gain this understanding, you need response data.

Few if any companies have response data readily available. Lack of computing power, however, does not explain why companies have not yet built the kinds of databases that can enhance their decision making. As one article on the topic affirms, "most manufacturers spend a lot of money on product sales data, but still can't determine the effects of changes in prices, features, or displays on sales."[4] The better explanation is that companies would rather rely on shortcuts, anecdotal evidence, conventional wisdom, aggregated data, and gut feelings to make their decisions than to make the additional mental investment required to uncover and understand these effects. Most of these companies have the capability to act, but not the desire.

You can generate response data in two ways: either you can make estimates based on your historical data, or you can survey your customers directly. We will discuss the first option now and the second option in the next chapter.

When companies choose to produce response data from their own historical data, they can rarely do so with straightforward or standardized analyses. Demand-planning software providers such as PROS Revenue Management, Zilliant, or Rapt have tried to fill this void by offering tools that make it easier for companies to collect and analyze status data, and generate response data, in a systematic way. But make no mistake—the key value of such software is that it helps you compile and transform data, but it will never entirely substitute for your judgment. Nor will it provide you with push-button insights. We have yet to see a software tool that would truly automate decision making.

The U.S. clothing retail chain Casual Male analyzed its historical data in order to determine the optimal time to discount fashion items. Conventional wisdom in the business dictated that retail stores cut the prices on bathing suits right after the July 4th weekend.

Steven Schwartz, Casual Male's senior vice president for planning, said that the company used to have "no clue whether we'd get a better margin by choosing one item over another."[5] He introduced Web-based pricing tools to analyze the chain's sales data across the country, and identified substantial regional variations in sales cycles. The chain's gross margins rose by 25 percent in the ensuing nine months, thanks in part to the new pricing system.[6]

A gain of 25 percent in gross margins represented a huge amount of additional profit for Casual Male. But the guidance provided by such heavy-duty number crunching is incomplete. It does not account for potential competitive reactions, nor does it allow you to estimate the effect of product and service variations you have not offered. Casual Male's software could help it calculate price response and price elasticities, but it could not help Casual Male infer whether a competitor would continue to follow conventional wisdom (one lower price, nationwide) or mimic Casual Male's approach in part or in whole. Likewise, if Casual Male sold only blue bathing suits, the model could not predict what would happen if it introduced red ones in certain regions, because it had no data on red bathing suits.

Estimating competitive reaction or the effect of product variations with internal data requires what we refer to as *expert judgment.* You gather the most knowledgeable and experienced staff from marketing, sales, customer service, and product development and use a structured approach to explore their assumptions on how customers would respond to certain changes to your marketing mix. Then you quantify their assumptions. The next case shows how to conduct such an analysis, step-by-step.

CASE STUDY

Issue: How to Fend off a Competitive Threat

Company: Cortez Chemical
Product: Soaps and detergents
Source: Simon-Kucher & Partners project

Cortez Chemical, a diversified and highly profitable manufacturer, was the market leader in cleaning products used in factories and on shop floors around the world. It found one of its key products in one business unit under threat from Chinese imports.[7] A mainland Chinese firm sold at wholesale prices 50 percent below what the company charged for its branded flagship product. Had the market shown strong growth, the company might have worried less. But it had long sensed that demand had slowed. The market had become mature.

Cortez's products relied on twenty-five-year-old technology. The company's pipeline was bone dry. Cortez could not innovate its way out of the problem, at least not in two years' time. In light of that constraint, Judith S., the business unit's manager, approached us with the following challenge: "Help me protect my market share and margins by figuring out how much I should cut prices by to fend off this threat." Cutting prices seemed not only intuitively sound, but also easy to implement, she argued. Momentum and political support for the idea had begun to grow.

Judith did not ask whether she should cut prices, but rather how much she should cut them. We suggested that she suppress her urge to act and instead step back to reexamine the situation. We asked her to do the following tasks:

- *Select the type of price that really drove her profit.* The appropriate price to consider in her case was her average net selling price (ANSP) to distributors. Both legally and practically, she had no control over the "street price," or the price at which the distributors sold her products to end customers.

- *Pick one realistic price point above the current ANSP level and one realistic one below it.* In Judith's case, the lower price point she selected corresponded to the ANSP before a price increase she had implemented a year earlier. The higher price corresponded to a price increase her division vice president had asked her to consider for the coming fiscal year. Theoretically she could have selected any price above and below. But the task made more sense to her when she could relate it to two other price points she and her team were familiar with.

- *Estimate the expected sales volume for each price point.* We asked her to estimate how her sales volume would change if she really did raise or lower her prices to the ones she defined earlier.

- *Estimate how key competitors would change their prices in response to each of these price points.* If she moved down, how would her new Chinese competitors respond? How would other competitors respond? Who would match the decrease, and who would rather hold prices steady at the expense of market share?

• *Repeat the steps for four additional lower price points.*

Initially she balked at the final two tasks, because she felt the answers she would give would amount to little more than wild guesses. But in reality, Judith—like her counterparts in any company—already had these numbers in her head. When she planned production for the upcoming year, analyzed unit sales from the previous year, or thought about why a price cut might be advantageous, she had already made similar estimates. All we had asked her to do was line them all up in a row. Figure 4-3 captures the results of her work.

FIGURE 4-3

What Judith filled out in the exercise

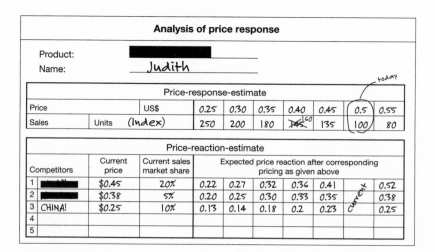

Source: Simon-Kucher & Partners

At first glance, this sheet seems to support Judith's point. Her current revenue (volume × price) is $50 million, or 100 million units at 50¢ apiece. (We have simplified all of the revenue numbers for illustrative purposes.) If she cut prices by half, she would boost her revenue to $62.5 million, or 250 million units at 25¢ each. But look closely at her assessment of how the competitors would respond. Because of her own industry experience and consultations with her colleagues, she thought that her main competitors would match her price cuts and in some cases exceed them. That meant that in some cases, Judith's products would be more expensive—relative to the competition—than they are currently. When she did the math, she saw immediately that these reactions would wipe out her expected volume gains and leave her with a volume similar to today's, but at a much lower price. This is the fundamental and dangerous consequence of competitive reaction that so many companies overlook. Competitors can and often will respond, thus neutralizing any gains you might have expected.

We have captured these effects in figure 4-4. We have indexed the revenue by setting Judith's current revenue to 100. Notice the difference in the two graphs. The revenue gains that a price decrease would promise her on paper (without competitive reaction) would actually turn into revenue losses if she took the anticipated competitive reaction into account. She could see that in this particular case, defending market share by cutting prices would be self-destructive. Because she was convinced that the Chinese company would match every price move, and then assumed her other competitors would as well, the small amount of market share she could defend or gain would not justify the money she would lose.

One year later, it became clear that the Chinese imports appealed only to a small subsegment of distributors and their extremely price-sensitive customers. Quality problems and shipping delays also

FIGURE 4-4

The revenue curves based on what Judith filled out

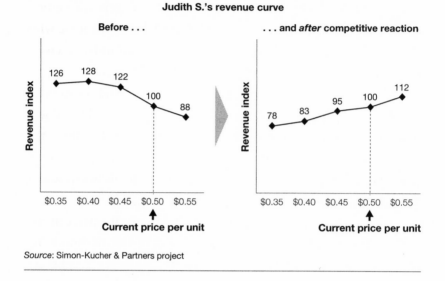

Judith S.'s revenue curve

Before . . .   . . . and *after* competitive reaction

Source: Simon-Kucher & Partners project

limited their appeal. The bulk of the market remained either unaware of these products entirely or unwilling to abandon their relationship with Judith's team. The threat may have looked daunting on paper, but it was minimal when measured against what ultimately counts: customer behavior.

This outcome verified her decision to leave prices steady and avoid a costly price war. The expert judgment method showed her, with her own data and on her own terms, that no response at all was by far the best alternative.

You can use the same steps with your own products to quickly quantify how much certain decisions will cost you or earn you. This approach also has a pleasant side effect. If you involve a larger team drawn from different functions in your company, you will see what happens when each participant puts his or her assumptions and market knowledge to work in a systematic way. The differences in people's estimates and in their rationales are important to note and discuss. By doing this exercise, people expose their assumptions to a much-needed challenge. The discussion stays on course when you let profits decide who has the best answer, in order to ensure objectivity.

We and our colleagues have conducted these kinds of exercises hundreds of times with companies throughout the world, and generally find that most companies' prices are too low. It follows that most companies have additional profit to capture through price and price alone. Chapter 7 shows in detail how companies have accomplished this.

But don't let the generalization that all companies can and should raise their prices degenerate into a blunt rule of thumb. You must evaluate your own case independently, using the insights and methods in this book. That is why we will not make blanket statements such as "85 percent of all companies have prices that are too low." They might sound compelling and meaningful, but in the end the only way you'll find out whether you are in the majority or the minority is to take an objective, thorough, and profit-oriented look at your whole business. We would rather have you do that than act on speculation.

The company in the next case, Kent Molding, used expert judgment to adjust its prices in certain customer segments. They found in some cases that their prices were indeed too high. Knowing this, they pulled off the rare trick of raising their profits in a mature market by lowering their prices.

Issue: Which Customers Have the Highest Profit Potential?

Company: Kent Molding
Product: Injection-molding services
Source: Simon-Kucher & Partners project

A smaller company, Kent Molding, took a similar approach to Cortez's, once it had access to better information about its customers and its profitability.[8] A provider of plastic injection-molding services, Kent worked primarily with manufacturers of food and personal care products. Its largest customer accounted for $10 million in annual sales, while the typical smaller customers accounted for around $1 million. The company historically had limited internal information. Its reports never went deeper than sales per customer. Once Kent made the effort to allocate costs accurately to individual customers and determine the profit contribution generated by each one, it began to notice the same kinds of discrepancies Northsan noticed in the case earlier in this chapter.

Kent's contribution margin at its third-largest customer came to just 10.5 percent. Its eighth-largest customer, however, had a contribution margin of 48.9 percent, which meant it generated over $1.5 million in contribution for Kent annually. This figure, in absolute terms, far outstripped the money Kent earned at the supposedly "more attractive" large customer.

Kent's cost structure had little to do with these enormous discrepancies that resulted from huge differences in prices and discounts from customer to customer. The information on customer-specific profit gave Kent the missing link it needed to recalibrate its entire approach to sales and customer selection. Kent could now identify the customers who had not paid a price commensurate with the services and support they received. It could also see which customers might have purchased more at lower prices and at the same time made Kent more profitable.

At the companies with the lowest contribution margins, Kent planned to raise prices and eliminate certain discounts in order to bring these customers in line with the rest of the market. If they defected, Kent would be willing to live with the loss. Other customers would either receive lower prices directly, or in most cases see the same price but with an increase in attention from customer service staff and technicians. Service levels became a powerful differentiator for Kent to keep these customers from switching and to defend its higher price levels.

Relying on response data generated through expert judgment, Kent turned theory into action. It did indeed raise prices across the board at customers with the lowest contribution margins. Kent had estimated how the customers would respond, so they knew that volume would drop and some customers would leave for the competition. Sales at one customer fell significantly, and another did indeed take its business elsewhere. Kent not only became more profitable, it could also reallocate the resources that customer used to consume.

After implementing this recalibration, Kent saw its revenue rise by 4.5 percent, from $67 million to $70 million. Gross profit increased by 5.7 percent, from $24.4 million to $25.8 million. This is not a trivial amount, especially for a small company. Had Kent tried to realize the same gains via cost cutting, it would have needed to eliminate around twenty-five jobs, or 10 percent of its workforce. It also achieved these sales and profit improvements in only six months, with little internal friction and minimal investment. Senior management made the mental investment, not the out-of-pocket one. The same moves on the cost side would have had serious repercussions on the company's morale. Its short-term profits would have also suffered as the company accounted for severance packages.

Summary

Your internal data on sales, volume, profit, and costs offers a rich source of information to help you shape better assumptions and make decisions that will increase profit. This data falls into two categories: status data and response data.

Status data provides you with the basic facts on what has happened: how much did you sell, to whom, and so on. The more finely you can break down the data, the more useful it becomes. Straightforward analyses, like those that Northsan and Kent Molding performed, can reveal where you earn the most profit and what market share you can afford to let go.

Response data provides with you information on "what would happen if?" It includes price elasticity and promotional effectiveness, which allow you to understand dynamics in your market and predict customer behavior.

You can use a tool called expert judgment to augment your internal data and generate demand and profit curves. These in turn help you understand how to make profitable marketing decisions confidently. Using this tool, managers can better decide how to pick their fights and the degree to which they should retaliate when threatened.

Internal data can provide you with plenty of fresh insights, but you will need to gather data directly from customers to test more sophisticated hypotheses. The next chapter describes these hypotheses and how to test them.

CHAPTER 5

Uncover Preferences
and Willingness to Pay

*The whole point of James was: don't be an ape! Think for yourself
along rational lines. Hypothesize, test against the evidence, never
accept that a question has been answered as well as it ever will be.*

—Michael Lewis, describing pioneering baseball analyst
Bill James, in his best-selling book *Moneyball.*[1]

WHEN YOU DRAW INSIGHTS from your internal data, as we discussed in the previous chapter, you face three limitations. First, you can model only past behavior, which means you need to use the past as a proxy for the future. Second, you cannot take potential competitive reactions into account in those cases when they would have a significant effect on customer behavior and therefore on your profit. Third, these analyses usually make sense only if you have a large set of data.

Make Sure Your Customer Research Is Hypothesis Driven and Focused

Because of these limitations, you will not be able to answer all of your market-related questions with your existing data. Likewise, you will have hypotheses that you can test directly only in the market with customers. If you must decide whether to add a new feature to your product, or how much a certain service is worth to customers, or how to convince customers to change the way they make their purchasing decisions, you will need to draw from a wider range of research options. Each of the methods shown in figure 5-1 is a valid, straightforward, and economical way to estimate customer responses, test hypotheses, or gain additional insights into customer behavior. They can help you answer questions such as:

- Why do your high-volume customers buy as much as they do?

- How stable is your relationship with them?

- Why do certain customers not buy more?

- What combination of changes—different products or services, better communication, other incentives—will spur small customers to buy more or allow you to earn more profit from large customers?

Regardless of how you proceed with external research, we strongly recommend choosing at least two methods. A distinct benefit of this approach is the ability to cross-check results, either because one method has yielded surprising or suspicious results or because you need the supplementary evidence to build buy-in for your conclusions. Complications often arise when you are doing consumer research; and in most cases, these complications have an uncanny knack for becoming apparent only after you have completed your data collection and have begun analyzing the data. In that case, the backup data provided by the additional methods and sources helps to clarify the results.

To show you how this works in detail, we will compare four distinct cases that we have chosen because the managers involved faced contrasting challenges in markets that have very different structures.

FIGURE 5-1

Appropriate applications of various research approaches

+ + = Great . . .
+ = Medium . . .
0 = Limited . . .
approach to gain insights for identifying profit opportunity

Methods		Sources: Internal — Historical data	Company experts	Sales force	Individual customers	External — Many customers (>30 per segment)
Directional	In-depth interviews		0	+	+ +	
	Expert judgment workshops		+ +	+		
	Focus groups				0	
	Structured questionnaire			+ +		+
	Statistical analysis	+ +		0		
Quantitative	Choice modeling					+ +
	In-market tests				0	+ +

Source: Simon-Kucher & Partners

The first case concerns a company that uses a catalog to sell low-involvement entertainment products to millions of individual consumers. The second involves a division of a company that supplies pigments to several hundred processing companies, many of which have sophisticated and informed purchasing departments. The third case shows how a distributor of around forty thousand industrial products reduced complexity in order to enable salespeople to assess customers' price sensitivities and make pricing decisions accordingly. The fourth shows how very large companies—in this case, a car company—approach customer research when the difference between good profit and peak profit could easily exceed $1 billion over the lifetime of the product.

Issue: Test Whether Certain Marketing Changes Would Increase Profits

Company: Bedrock Entertainment
Product: Toys, games, and educational products
Source: Simon-Kucher & Partners project

The product and marketing managers developed and prioritized several hypotheses that determined where they might earn additional profits.[2] The managers settled on three: they could differentiate their product offering by customer segment; they could introduce shipping charges for certain products; and they could communicate their product value better in the catalog in order to spur sales.

In the spirit of chapter 4 we started with statistical analysis of their historical data. As you might imagine, a mail order company has massive and complex databases. But as you also might expect after reading the previous chapter, the task of consolidating this data into one useful database took much longer than the company had anticipated. We needed over four weeks to combine accurate data on net prices and sales volumes by product into one set.

A series of cluster analyses allowed us to confirm the project's first hypothesis. Bedrock had four distinct customer segments, each with very different buying patterns and willingness to pay. The product teams developed new product offerings for each segment, which they subsequently tested on a large scale in order to gather response data. (We explore segmentation and product adjustments in greater detail in chapter 6.)

Historical data, however, can reveal only so much. We were unable to address the other hypotheses using internal data alone. That data could not tell us whether customers would accept shipping and handling charges on certain products, nor could it show how customers might respond to better communication. To test these hypotheses would require response data, which in this case meant primary research with customers.

The idea of a shipping charge became a flashpoint for controversy among Bedrock's senior managers. The proponents said, "We can get away with it," because customers would barely notice the nominal charge and would appreciate the rationale behind it. If most direct-to-customer businesses already charged for shipping, Bedrock should as well.

The opponents said the charge would "kill the business" because it would violate an unwritten pact between the company and its customers. A company built on free shipping would appear mercenary and greedy if it tacked on a shipping charge, no matter how small or well hidden on the order form.

Who do you think is correct?

Fortunately, both sides agreed to settle the argument in the court of customer opinion. Bedrock would conduct a controlled market test. From a mechanical standpoint, testing the shipping charge proved to be straightforward. The company could run a controlled test in the market at little cost by making minor changes to upcoming catalogs. Despite this superficial simplicity, though, the success of the experiment depended on three factors: gaining explicit sign-off from management on the experiment's design; defining the control group; and defining a way to measure and interpret the results.

All stakeholders need to sign off explicitly on any customer research you design. You run a great risk with any form of market research or market test if someone decides to challenge the design later because the results did not come out in their favor. Gaining sign-off up front minimizes this risk. It allows you to spend your time discussing and interpreting results when the survey is done, instead of bickering about methodologies.

The second step is to define the control group. When you conduct a "live" market test, you must compare the results of your test group with those of a control group. Both groups should have the same composition. Comparing a test group of customers from North Dakota with a control group in California would make no sense, because you cannot distinguish whether your test explains the differences in results between the test and control groups, or other factors played a role.

Finally, you need unanimous agreement on how to measure and interpret test results. In this case, we defined two easily observable metrics. We would compare the numbers of orders in each group and the number of items per order. Because each metric in the test group could either be higher, lower, or the same as in the control group, the test would have nine possible outcomes. For example, if orders and items per order were either the same or higher in the test group, it would indicate that the shipping charge slipped in under the customers' radar screens. They did not seem to mind, and the company would capture an incremental profit because the shipping charge was extra revenue on every order. (Costs, obviously, would stay the same, because Bedrock needed to ship the items anyway.) If either metric were lower in the test group, it would indicate some form of resistance to the idea. People either refused to order entirely or ordered fewer items.

Keep in mind that an experiment in a small section of the market cannot produce any insights on the potential competitive reaction. The test either goes unnoticed or is regarded as an experiment that does not warrant a reaction. Price optimization software that "infuses" price variation through experiments in the marketplace is therefore a very dangerous tool: the outcome of the software test results may suggest that you should cut your price. But if you then cut prices nationwide—a decision that no competitor could interpret as "just an experiment"—you will inevitably force your competition to react.

Bedrock tested the shipping idea in two successive catalog cycles because achieving an objective, repeatable result would reinforce the conclusions of the first test. The second test did indeed provide that confirmation. Metrics were lower for the test group than for the control group each time. The idea of introducing a shipping charge died. Both opponents and proponents breathed a sigh of relief, knowing that the objective evidence from the market test had just prevented Bedrock from using gut feeling to make a decision that would have sacrificed millions of dollars in profits had they guessed wrong.

The final hypothesis explored whether better communication would increase sales. Testing that hypothesis in the market would have generated much less controversy, but would have presented greater mechanical challenges and required a major investment to redesign upcoming catalogs. As an alternative, we agreed with Bedrock to conduct a series of focus groups.

Having two decades of experience in conducting focus groups, we suggest that you conduct them only if you expect more input from customers in a group than from speaking with them one on one. In other words, a focus group works only if one idea truly leads to another and the output of a group discussion is richer than the individual input. Nonetheless, you must weigh this advantage against the risks. Strong personalities can dominate a focus group discussion and strongly bias it. It is also very difficult in some focus groups to distinguish between consensus and resignation among the participants.

The results of Bedrock's four separate focus groups helped reaffirm our second and final piece of advice on focus groups: you must have realistic expectations about the results. As expected, some focus groups liked Bedrock's new concepts, while others didn't. As a by-product of the very fruitful discussions, Bedrock did gain some fresh, useful insights into how its customers perceive its catalogs. But the actual object of the focus group—to test specific ideas that would improve communication—revealed no pattern and no immediately actionable result. Bedrock could infer that a few of the ideas had little chance of success, but could not pinpoint any clear "winners."

As a rule of thumb, the less exploratory and more specific your task, the more you should lean toward personal customer interviews based on a structured questionnaire instead of conducting focus groups.

The next case, involving the pigment supplier Kleber Enterprises, illustrates the use of other methods shown in figure 5-1, including choice modeling.

CASE STUDY

Issue: Test New Forms of Customer Segmentation

Company: Kleber Enterprises
Product: Pigments
Source: Simon-Kucher & Partners project

Similarly to the Bedrock project, this project began with work to develop and prioritize hypotheses to test. In Kleber's case, the team felt strongly that it could capture additional profit by first establishing a better customer segmentation, then differentiating products, services, and prices according to that segmentation.[3]

Unlike Bedrock, Kleber had two distinct operating divisions. The regional group served fifteen hundred small customers, while the national group focused on fifty key accounts. Given this breakdown, a large-scale survey of regional customers would make sense. This raises a question that has become the topic of endless scholarly debates: how large should your sample size be? We have found that in research in industrial markets, a sample size of forty to sixty respondents per group or segment works quite well in most cases. You define these segments in advance. Let's say you want to understand the buying behavior of customers who buy less than $100,000 of product from you per year. You would need interviews with forty to sixty such customers in order to draw any valid conclusions. Surveys of customers in business-to-business markets tend to have an incidence rate of between 5 and 20 percent, which means that in the best case roughly one out of every five customers you contact agrees to an interview. In the best case, we could expect to get as many as three hundred of the regional customers to participate.

The methods you plan to use in the interview usually determine how you should conduct the interview. Conducting surveys over the Internet has become very popular because it is cheap and fast. The authors have had good success with Internet-based interviews, though response quality tends to decline if the questions are complex and challenging or especially if the questionnaire takes more than forty-five minutes to complete. The one disadvantage is the lack of opportunity to interact personally with the respondent. If you feel that interaction is necessary but still want to keep costs at a minimum, telephone interviews with supporting material available online or on paper offer a good compromise. With Kleber we agreed to conduct one hundred fifty computer-aided personal interviews designed to last between thirty and forty-five minutes.

The interviews with Kleber's customers involved pricing, which raised yet another question that has intrigued the academic community over the last fifty years: how does one measure value perception and price sensitivity?

Some of the standard methods for direct questioning on prices ("Would you buy product X at $19.95? At 14.95?") have developed systematic errors over the last few decades. As a result, these research methods generally underestimate a customer's true willingness to pay. Consumers have developed a fine-tuned conditioning and sensitivity toward price that they lacked at the time these methods first gained usage in the 1950s. This is particularly true of industrial companies with dedicated professional purchasing departments. The nature of the direct questions only reinforces this systematic error, because it overly sensitizes the respondent to the price.

Another method for direct questioning involves asking customers what kinds of prices or price structures they prefer. This kind of research often yields obvious conclusions about what customers prefer, but gives little insight into what customers would actually pay. Of course heavy users prefer flat rates. Of course long-distance travelers prefer price structures that offer greater discounts or bonuses for longer trips. But the relevant questions for you are how much will they actually *pay*? And will they still buy even when you use a price structure that is not their first preference? Only an indirect questioning method can reveal these answers.

Indirect methods such as adaptive conjoint analysis (ACA) or discrete choice modeling (DCM) offer a more precise gauge of willingness to pay and of product value. We call them indirect methods because they do not vary price alone but other product attributes as well, so that one can gauge willingness to pay indirectly. Each method strives to confront the respondents with realistic buying decisions and forces them to make trade-offs between alternatives. Without wading too deeply into the methodological details, we can outline some of the strengths and weaknesses of each approach. Discrete choice modeling works best in established markets where the set of competitors is well defined. It is typically the method of choice for companies looking to identify new profit opportunities buried within existing products. Adaptive conjoint analysis is less difficult to set up and use, but this method is generally less precise in simulating the realities of the marketplace.[4]

The proliferation of low-cost software packages from companies like Sawtooth have turned DCM and ACA into inexpensive commodities. But cheap access to the tools does not guarantee that you will obtain useful, valid results. The plug-and-play nature of each method makes them look deceptively simple, and designing trade-offs for your customers to make presents an intriguing, perhaps even fun challenge. In reality it takes years of experience to set up an indirect research design properly, particularly when it includes your most important variable, price. A survey including ACA or DCM must be very economically designed, because these methods can quickly exhaust even the most enthusiastic respondent. The risk of using an improperly designed study is especially acute in an industrial market, where you have a smaller number of customers and no second chance to conduct another study. It's one strike and you're out. We suggest that if you decide to use DCM or ACA, allow an expert to design the study for you, especially when the pool of potential respondents is relatively small (as in an industrial market).

Conducting this kind of research also requires a commitment of resources that sometimes catches a company off guard. You need to consider the cost of recruiting respondents and conducting the interviews, as well as the time to develop the questionnaire, conduct the survey, and analyze the data you've collected. For Kleber, this entire process consumed twelve weeks, evenly split among questionnaire development, surveying, and analysis of the data.

The cost for an individual interview can range from $20 to $500, depending on how you conduct the interview, the degree of specialization of the industry or customer group, and whether you need to provide the respondent with an incentive. If visiting the pool of potential interviewees requires international travel, the costs rise even further. At the low end, a survey of consumers on the Internet could cost $20 to $30 per recruited interview, with no incentive necessary. At the high end—for example, for highly specialized industries or products—a computer-aided personal interview could cost $250 to conduct, plus $100 to $250 face value in incentives.

The interviews for Kleber cost around $340 per interview to conduct, including the average incentive of $140. If you plan to interview between fifty and three hundred respondents, you should budget at least three weeks to conduct the entire survey, the "field phase." The Kleber study actually took four weeks because of initial difficulties in making appointments with customers.

It also took around four weeks to develop the right questionnaire and gain explicit sign-off from all stakeholders within Kleber management. That sounds like a long time until you actually examine what really goes on when complex questionnaires get developed.

The process usually goes smoothly. But a questionnaire making its way through corporate management is often treated like a piece of legislation winding its way through Congress. People you have never met before will get wind of the fact that someone is about to conduct a customer survey. They will insist that the survey include all sorts of questions whose answers may be fascinating but completely irrelevant to the hypotheses you would like to test. In the worst case, people who don't get their way will filibuster at meetings to impede your progress. When you find that you are spending more time keeping things *out* of the survey than building them in, it is time to step back and make everyone clear about the questionnaire's objectives and the precise hypotheses you intend to investigate.

A questionnaire requiring this level of investment and quality also deserves to undergo adequate testing before you program the final version and begin the field phase. This also consumes considerable time but will help you avoid wasting the respondents' time. Advertising pioneer and market research advocate David Ogilvy once described an encounter he had with a survey he had written himself. He thought the questions made sense until he tried to answer them spontaneously in a real-life situation: "I was accosted by an inter-viewer and asked questions which I had written two days before. They were impossible to answer."[5] If a question's phrasing risks con-fusing the respondent, it will undermine the quality of your data. Keep your questions as simple and direct as possible. Avoid what we call *professor questions*, which ramble on using erudite phrasings, jar-gon, and loads of unnecessary detail. You are trying to gather infor-mation from customers, not give them a pop quiz.

After the raw data comes in from the interviews, it takes an aver-age of four additional weeks to consolidate it, analyze it, and draw valid conclusions. The patience and cooperation of the Kleber man-agement team paid off. The survey revealed four distinct segments that formed the basis of a major overhaul of its entire commercial strategy. By adapting products and services to each segment, and aligning its organization with those changes, Kleber expected its re-turn on sales to increase from 7 percent to as much as 10 percent. This change represented a huge pool of potential profit for a com-pany in a highly competitive business with declining profit margins. We treat segmentation in greater detail in chapter 6.

The national division effort, which ran concurrently, required an entirely different approach because of the small pool of custom-ers. A survey with indirect methods such as ACA and DCM would have been impractical. Assuming normal incidence across their fifty key accounts, we would have considered ten interviews a success, far below the level required for an indirect research method.

To provide a proxy for the customer input, we conducted a series of in-depth interviews with Kleber salespeople and managers di-rectly involved in negotiating contracts with these customers. We refer to this approach as a *deal postmortem analysis*. Time was the major resource commitment for Kleber in this phase. You should plan on one person-day for setting up, conducting, and analyzing each separate talk. Participants should also make available as much documentation as possible, including copies of draft contracts, final contracts, subsequent amendments, and internal and external correspondence. This additional information helps in reconstructing the negotiating process and looking for ways to optimize it.

This *deal postmortem* approach has three primary objectives: discover best practices to share with the rest of the organization, identify pitfalls in negotiations, and gather information on patterns in customer behavior. In Kleber's case, we identified several best practices, which have been incorporated into a more rigorous process for negotiating future contracts. The inferences on customer behavior enabled us to assign most of the key accounts to the segments identified in the large-scale study with the smaller, regional customers.

As we describe in detail in the next section, keep in mind that the goal of the deal postmortem is not internal espionage. When you conduct a deal postmortem yourself, focus first on what the sales teams have done well, not on their shortcomings. If the impression arises that this exercise is about blame rather than improvement, you will end up wasting your time. No one will cooperate with you. We stress again the point we made at the end of chapter 1. You can find and retrieve your hidden profits only if you focus on the profit itself, not how it came to be hidden. You are on a profit hunt, not a witch hunt.

Transform Your Sales and Service Forces into Information Sources

A question many organizations struggle with is how to draw out useful information from the salespeople and service technicians. It makes sense that the salespeople or service technicians have information that could have an impact on your decisions. The amount of time they spend with customers is usually an order of magnitude larger than the time managers and executives spend with customers.

This leads to an interesting paradox in how companies gather information on their customers. The sales force spends most of any given day in direct customer contact, yet when the marketing department wants to know something about customers, it conducts an external survey with them and interprets the results on its own. Marketing teams defend this by citing a level of uncertainty in what they hear from the salespeople. They wonder how objective salespeople really are. If salespeople keep all their information in their head and never write anything down, how complete and unbiased are the stories they tell?

In any event, your sales force is a repository of valuable raw information. The relevant question is, How do you have a conversation with your sales force to extract that information successfully? Our first suggestion is not to have a conversation at all, but rather a structured interview, much as the kind that Kleber conducted with its regional customers. Give them sets of brief questions that they can answer quickly. The more quantitative questions you have, the better. Phrase your open-ended questions carefully, or the process will degenerate into an exchange of war stories, either their own or others they've collected over time. At the same time, make sure that you ask only the questions that the sales force can answer best. Conducting these interviews is the fine art of not wasting your interview partner's time. See if you can find the answers from other sources like written documentation, product literature, trade magazines, and so on before you pose the question to someone personally.

The idea of extracting information from your sales team in this manner and the idea of doing market research are not mutually exclusive. Granted, if you conduct a survey of four hundred customers with interviews lasting two hours each, you get eight hundred hours of insight into what customers think, in a way where you control the course of the discussion. This work is usually worth the investment, if done as described in the previous section: hypothesis driven and focused.

The focused eight hundred hours of customer interviews do yield valuable information. The pity is that many people invest too little in unlocking valuable information from those thousands or even millions of person-hours your salespeople or service technicians have spent with customers. This applies in particular to service technicians, who may have neither the patience nor the motivation to put feedback into terms that marketing or design teams can easily digest. The founder of a leading machinery company described this misalignment: "Service technicians' feedback can be quite unpleasant. They clearly state the difficulties they encountered, what has gone wrong, what should be changed and improved. They have an excellent understanding of such problems . . . but in most firms the technicians don't have enough opportunities to bring their complex experience directly to designers. And technicians dislike having to present written reports."[6] A structured interview, as described earlier, would meet the technicians more than halfway and provide marketing and design teams with an additional, albeit indirect perspective from customers.

The following case shows how input from the sales force not only played a major role in developing pricing recommendations, but also helped ensure their implementation's success. The sales force had a sense of pride and ownership, not only because it contributed to the process, but also because management took its input seriously and incorporated it into the final results.

An industrial distributor we'll call Kinston carries over forty thousand products, which a team of more than twenty thousand employees sells to contractors, shops, and companies in over one hundred countries.

Issue: Determine Price Elasticities

Company: Kinston
Product: Distribution of industrial supplies
Source: Simon-Kucher & Partners project

Kinston faced the same marketplace pressures we have discussed throughout the book.[7] Customers had become more sophisticated. They challenged suppliers' claims of differentiation and insisted on steeper and steeper discounts. As competition intensified, customers increasingly made price—not service or quality—the centerpiece of every negotiation. Already a very efficient operation with best-in-class logistics, Kinston saw little room to make profit gains through additional cost cutting.

Despite these pressures, Kinston tried to preserve a price premium thanks to its presumed competitive advantages in product range, technical competence, logistics, and brand name. Profits still declined, however, as margins became tighter. The company saw an urgent need to raise margins, or at the very least prevent a further decline. Where did the company have realistic opportunities to increase profits?

For the first time in its history, Kinston undertook a quantitative examination of the price dynamics in its markets. To do this properly, it needed a way to estimate price elasticity and understand the shape of its profit curve. How do you figure out the price elasticities and draw profit curves for forty thousand products? Doing it product by product is, of course, absurd.

To accelerate the process, Kinston needed to sort both its customers and products together into sensible, relatively homogeneous groups. In the end, Kinston classified the products into thirty-nine groups. Teams of salespeople met in workshops and discussion rounds to give their best estimate of how demand would respond to price changes, using the same expert judgment method that companies such as Cortez and Kent used in chapter 4. From the demand curves, the project team could calculate price elasticities, which were later made accessible via a special program on each salesperson's laptop.

Kinston then went two steps further by using other approaches we've discussed in chapters 4 and 5. It conducted a thorough analysis of historical transaction data, which yielded another set of price elasticities complementary to the ones drawn from the expert judgment of the sales force. Finally, it conducted a survey with one hundred customers. The design resembled the one Kleber used, but Kinston limited the scope to a handful of representative product groups.

Generating three sets of price elasticities from three distinct approaches is an extreme but powerful example of our recommendation to use multiple methods and sources when you launch your search for additional profit. Armed with this bounty of information, Kinston could provide precise guidance to salespeople on what discount thresholds would endanger profitability.

To encourage adoption of the new system, Kinston overhauled the way it compensated its salespeople. We describe the changes they made in chapter 9, which we have devoted entirely to the topic of sales incentives for salespeople, agents, and channel partners.

Keep Customer Research Investment in Line with the Stakes Involved

Kinston's incremental profit, in absolute dollars, was much higher than the amounts Bedrock or Kleber expected to achieve. But it is still only a fraction of the amount of profit at stake when a car company launches a new model or a drug company launches a new pharmaceutical product with blockbuster potential. In this final section, we describe the approach taken when the additional profits can amount to billions, not millions of dollars.

CASE STUDY

Issue: How to Find the Most Profitable Price for a New Product

Company: Jetson Motors
Product: New vehicle
Source: Simon-Kucher & Partners project

In the 1990s, Jetson Motors introduced a new model design. Just as Chrysler caused a sensation when it introduced the minivan, the company hoped it could establish a new vehicle category that would appeal to drivers who wanted flexibility and functionality in a small, affordable package.[8]

If the carmaker followed conventional wisdom, the price positioning would be clear. The price for the vehicle should lie under the psychological threshold of $15,000. The company could manufacture the car profitably at that price level. The company also found the idea intriguing that it could offer a vehicle in that price range for the first time. Its least expensive model at that time sold for more than $20,000. Finally, that price would give the new car a premium of around 9 percent over the best-selling competitor car in that segment. This seemed consistent with the brand premium it normally enjoyed.

All the pieces fell logically into place. The company aimed for a price of $14,750 and hoped to sell out its initial annual capacity of three hundred thousand units. Then the doubts emerged.

How much sense did it make to follow the conventional wisdom for an unconventional car? What value did the company's brand really have in this new segment? The company had few indicators to work with because it had never tapped this segment before. How much would customers really be willing to pay for the new design and convenience features? Even more fundamentally, what percentage of consumers would really care about the new design and features at all?

The more such questions arose, the shakier the price of $14,750 became. The company decided to test its hypotheses about features and prices directly with potential customers. The ensuing study focused on the car's design and features. Potential customers watched a video that demonstrated the vehicle's advantages they may have otherwise struggled to visualize clearly. The video was an effective surrogate for the actual experience of visiting a car dealer and investigating the model. A combination of two indirect methods was used to quantify customers' expected behavior: the DCM method was used to determine the choice behavior between the new car and competing models. The ACA method helped sort out what the customers would actually be willing to pay for the individual features. This data was used to construct a complex decision support model that simulated various market scenarios: using the preference data from the survey, Jetson could input certain product configurations for its own new vehicle as well as for the competition's vehicles, and the model would predict the associated market shares. What they saw surprised everybody, not least the carmaker's marketing and technical experts, or "car guys."

- *Polarization.* The new design strongly polarized customers. Roughly one-quarter were true fans, the remaining three-quarters of respondents categorically rejected it. It became clear that the final price should reflect only the fans' input, because only they would even seriously considering purchasing the vehicle.

- *Willingness to pay.* The fans' willingness to pay exceeded the company's expectations. They found both the functionality and the brand highly attractive.

- *Resulting recommendation.* Our project team recommended a price of $15,500, which ignored the whole "threshold" wisdom entirely. We also forecast that the company would still sell out its full capacity at that price.

The carmaker followed the recommendation. In the first year, it sold 293,000 units. This level of capacity utilization (98 percent) essentially represents full capacity, considering that this was the first production year. By earning an extra $750 per car and still selling 293,000 units per year, the company generated an additional $220 million in profits per year.

The more valid information about customers and the quantification of their willingness to pay made the difference. Had the company not undertaken the study, it would never have realized *ahead of the launch* that its new car would touch off this "love-hate" split in the car-buying public. Even with the study's results, they still would have overlooked substantial profit if they had lumped these two diametrically opposed customer groups into one pot and looked at overall averages. Using any form of aggregates and averages would have led them far astray, as we discussed in chapter 3.

Through this study, the company also saw the real-life effects of another kind of threshold that very few managers take into account consciously: namely, how high a price premium they can charge while maintaining the same positioning against competitors. Until a company crosses that threshold, it will lose hardly any customers at all when it makes relatively small increases to its price premium. Cross that threshold, however, and the effect on volume is dramatic.

Customers abandon the product because the price difference—relative to your competition—has gone from high to crass.

The increase to $15,500 raised the vehicle's price premium against the main competitive product from around 9 percent to over 14 percent. Given that customers' only other reference point for this brand would be a much more expensive vehicle, the shift of 5 percentage points in the relative price seemed acceptable.

Summary

Internal data analyses are powerful but often inadequate or inappropriate to test certain hypotheses about your customers. These fundamental hypotheses include why customers behave the way they do and how they would respond to product and service changes. You can test these concepts reliably only through research with customers. This research can include market tests and customer surveys.

If you conduct a market test, as Bedrock did in the case in this chapter, make sure you have met two criteria: a clear-cut way to interpret the results and a control group to allow objective and relevant comparisons

If you test customers' willingness to pay, you should use a range of methods rather than relying on just one. You should use at least one indirect pricing method, such as DCM or ACA. Only methods such as these allow you to quantify the trade-offs your customers make and express those trade-offs reliably in terms of dollars and cents.

Regardless of which approach you take, make sure that your investments remain pragmatic and in line with the amount of profit at stake. The greater the stakes, the more valuable it is to have a high degree of precision on your customers' willingness to pay. Car companies and pharmaceutical companies often have more than $1 billion at risk when they make marketing decisions, which justifies their heavy investments in complex customer research and analysis.

Having the right combination of internal and external data will prepare you to start capturing the additional profit you deserve. That effort begins in the next chapter, which shows you how to rethink and redirect your marketing mix.

CHAPTER 6

Optimize Your Marketing Mix
to Capture the Highest
Additional Profit

Knowing what to measure and how to measure it
makes a complicated world much less so.
—Steven D. Levitt and Stephen J. Dubner, *Freakonomics*[1]

B Y N O W you have gained an understanding of how to find and quantify your additional profit potential. Starting with this chapter, we will show you how to extract it.

Getting profits back from your customers involves wielding the full power in your marketing mix: product, promotion, place, and price. As discussed in previous chapters, your progress in this effort will depend on your willingness to challenge the "facts" that have historically guided your thinking, and replace them if warranted. This chapter focuses on the ideas and techniques you can use to improve the first three of those elements in your marketing mix. Chapter 7 focuses exclusively on the fourth element, price, which deserves a more detailed treatment because of the critical role it plays in the profit equation.

We begin the chapter with a discussion of segmentation and then discuss how to adapt your product and service portfolio to align it with your segments. Finally, we show how the nature and timing of your promotional activities can help you attract more customers, not inadvertently drive them into your competitors' arms.

Segment Your Customers by Preferences and Willingness to Pay

Effective customer segmentation accomplishes four things: it enables you to divide customers into relatively homogeneous groups; it also allows you to describe these groups in quantitative terms and easily identify the segment a given customer belongs to, so that you can measure, assign, and monitor them; it ensures that you have the sales channels and consistent communication messages to reach the groups; and finally, it creates groups that match up with the products and services your company can actually provide. If you can't act on segmentation, after all, why bother?

Contrast that with the most basic form of segmentation still in use at many companies. It combines two things: where customers are located and how much they purchase. Similar to the cost-plus method for pricing described in chapter 3, this approach to segmentation is a convenient shortcut of the corporate world that offers managers some semblance of guidance. It is a vestige of the days before computerization, when unit sales constituted most of the data that a manager had available. Under those circumstances, what else would you use as the basis for segmentation? These managers did the best they could with their limited resources.

Like cost-plus pricing, volume-based segmentation has a quantitative feel, makes use of readily available information, and is easy to communicate and understand. Until you dig deeper, this method of segmentation even seems to meet the criteria laid out two paragraphs ago. But like all such shortcuts, it has a fundamental draw-back. In this case, volume-based segmentations may have little or nothing to do with the real source of your profits: customer prefer-ences and your customers' willingness to pay for certain products and services. Ultimately, your incremental profit comes directly from your customers. It is profit you have yet to claim. It makes perfect sense for you to build your marketing mix around customers' prefer-ences and willingness to pay.

Nowadays, managers have both a wealth of data and the means to analyze this data quickly and reliably. Yet many of them continue to use the same segmentation technique their grandparents did. Geography and purchase volume may have once been a useful proxy for customers' preferences and willingness to pay, but all too often we have seen that this link broke long ago. Such a segmentation tech-nique may help managers characterize the current state of their mar-kets, but it provides them with no insights into what their markets could or should look like. It does not give them insights they can act on quickly to make more money. In other words, it does not help them decide which customers they shouldn't serve as intensively and which customers will pay more for certain products and services that others don't want as badly.

If you segment your market according to customers' preferences and willingness to pay rather than solely on geography and volume, you will become aware of how you can adapt your offering of prod-ucts and services to match each segment's preferences and capture that profit. This new focus will allow you to deploy your sales teams and marketing dollars more effectively. In some cases, that could mean offering services at a different level of intensity or adding addi-tional product and services variations. In other cases, it could mean restricting your focus to a select group of segments, then shrink-ing your product and service portfolio by eliminating what you no longer need. You can consult the competition map developed in chapter 2 for additional guidance on what products you could potentially shed. In all cases, though, you will have a segmentation you can act on profitably.

The next two cases demonstrate how a company can abandon shortcut approaches and segment its customers according to their preferences. The second case also shows how a company can challenge its conventional wisdom and take this process one step further by refining its segmentation to reflect customers' willingness to pay. Cases later in the chapter describe how these more advanced segmentations have helped companies decide whether to bundle or unbundle their product offerings, using profit potential as their guide.

CASE STUDY

Issue: Develop a New Segmentation

Company: Earnhardt Electronics
Product: Small electronic motors
Source: Simon-Kucher & Partners project

Earnhardt Electronics is a leading supplier of small electronic devices used in cars, household appliances, consumer electronics, and climate control equipment.[2] Traditionally, the company had a regional sales organization—that is, its representatives covered all customers in a certain region. This way of organizing the sales teams resulted less from a response to customer preferences than from a desire to save costs and maximize effective selling time. Engineers by training, Earnhardt sales representatives often required considerable time and coordination on-site with a potential customer in order to sell their complex, often highly customized products. The company felt that this closeness to the customer, on its own, gave it an advantage.

In the late 1990s, two changes in customer preferences caught Earnhardt off guard. First, customers complained that their technical requirements had become more sophisticated. Second, they started to demand industry-specific solutions instead of the often time-consuming and costly customization of standard products. Earnhardt's research and development teams met the challenge effectively, as did its manufacturing group. But these two shifts threatened to render its old regional segmentation of customers and the corresponding sales organization obsolete. Customers in the sales regions were not homogeneous. Earnhardt could not reach them with one consistent set of messages and channels, nor could it develop a single package of products and services to serve them.

It needed to develop a new segmentation and, at the same time, upgrade the competencies of its sales representatives. Discussions with customers in the four key industries (automotive, appliances, consumer electronics, and climate control) clearly revealed that the customers wanted more than just technical information from sales representatives. They expected knowledge of market and consumer trends, a deep understanding of competitive offerings, and information on innovations from other countries, especially Japan and Korea. Earnhardt had confidence that its sales representatives could accomplish this for one industry. But expecting the sales reps to stay abreast of four industries simultaneously with the same high level of competence, depth, and breadth was clearly unrealistic. Fortunately, many sales representatives had already begun to specialize, albeit unsystematically, because they happened to have a higher concentration of one or two industries in their territories.

Earnhardt replaced the regional sales organization with an industry-specific organization. Because of the sales reps' existing knowledge base and experience, the reorganization went smoothly and took only about four months to complete. The company knew that the new organization erased all of the perceived cost advantages of the old one. Some sales reps now needed to cover the entire country, which drove up travel costs and reduced effective selling time. But the benefits of the new system far outweighed these disadvantages. The new segmentation based on customer industry helped Earnhardt quickly restore its double-digit growth rates within one year after implementation.

You may argue that Earnhardt may have waited too long to make its change. It is hard to estimate precisely how much money it sacrificed by missing early signs from customers or by postponing change until the pressure from the customer side finally manifested itself in significant lost business. One impediment, though, was the company's desire to preserve its focus on the apparent cost efficiencies of a regional sales force rather than letting profit potential serve as its guide.

In contrast to Earnhardt, other industrial companies have already made the move toward a segmentation based on industry focus. We are hardly trying to sell you industry-based segmentation as a new idea. Nor are we claiming that industry-based segmentation is a must for all companies. We once worked for a client that had introduced a divisional, industry-oriented company structure in the late 1980s. Ten years later, by means of a large customer survey in many countries, we were actually able to prove that an old-fashioned regional organization made much more sense, because it offered a better way to capture incremental profit.

The next step involves taking customers' willingness to pay into account. How much additional profit can companies identify and capture if they segment customers according to that important piece of information?

Reshape Your Product Offering According to Customers' Willingness to Pay

If you segment your existing and potential customers according to preferences and willingness to pay, you are likely to find that you can serve some of the resulting segments more competitively and profitably than you can others. In the short term, you may be better off if you muster the courage to let the latter segments go, especially if they match up with cells on the competition map in which you do not hold the position of comparative advantage. You may devote fewer resources to them or even ignore them entirely. This is easy to say, but hard to implement if you have decision makers in your organization who still subscribe to a culture of aggression or acquiescence. Therefore, some of the points from earlier chapters bear repeating here.

As we said in the first chapter, businesses will always need to explore opportunities to enter new markets and develop new products. They need to determine how they can successfully move beyond their core and into adjacent market areas.[3] Those explorations, however, take considerable time and investment. Someday, years from now, you may have the new offering that allows you to compete profitably in the other markets, or "adjacencies." The time frame for the techniques, measures, and actions in this book, however, is measured in months, not years. The Earnhardt case showed that a company can redeploy its sales and service teams in a few months and realize an immediate profit improvement.

A similar time frame applies to changes in your product portfolio. Eliminating products and streamlining a portfolio goes much faster than the development and introduction of new products. An effective but often tricky way to do this is to bundle or unbundle your products.

If your job involves crafting such bundles for customers, we are sure that you would love to have overarching, hard-and-fast rules on when to bundle and when to focus on separate products. One group of academics undertook the exhaustive and exhausting task of finding those "easy rules" for bundling and declared it futile: "There are no general or simple rules [for bundling]."[4] Nonetheless, they did note that companies that attempt to create bundles find that "the optimal solution depends on the distribution of customers' willingness to pay."[5]

By segmenting customers according to their willingness to pay, companies can determine whether bundling or unbundling a product is more profitable. The automobile manufacturer Callisto Motors found an additional profit of over $50 million by examining who would pay for a certain option included in a premium model.[6]

CASE STUDY

Issue: Whether to Unbundle a Product Offering

Company: Callisto Motors
Product: Televisions in cars
Source: Simon-Kucher & Partners project

When automobile manufacturers began equipping more and more of their premium cars with television sets, they usually integrated the TV into the screen of the navigation system that customers bought as optional equipment. One manufacturer offered the TV function at no additional charge because it considered it a nice add-on feature to the navigation system.

As the company prepared to launch a new model, the marketing team debated whether to continue offering the feature for free or to add a separate charge. When the team surveyed customers, it uncovered sharp differences in opinion and in knowledge of the feature:

- Many customers had no idea they had the TV function already integrated and available.

- Most who did know of its existence used it very sparingly.

- Only about 10 percent of the customers used the feature regularly and considered it a "must" in their car.

Because of this information, the company decided to discontinue the TV-for-free option. They would instead price it separately. This effectively unbundled the function from the navigation system. Using additional data from the study, they estimated the optimal price at around $1,400. The economics of that decision looked like the following:

- *Segment.* At a price of $1,400, around 10 percent of all buyers of the new model would purchase the TV. The vast majority of these customers generally purchased fully loaded vehicles anyway, without really examining what these special option packages included.

- *Revenue.* The company expected to sell around four hundred thousand units of its new model over its entire life cycle. An uptake of 10 percent for the TV meant forty thousand buyers and an additional $56 million in revenues.

- *Volume.* The company felt the probability that customers would decide against buying the new model because of the unbundling of the TV was very low. Volume losses would be minimal at worst. Remember that 90 percent of all buyers had no interest in the TV anyway.

- *Profit.* The marginal cost for the TV function is low. That meant that most of the $56 million in extra revenue amounted to pure extra profit.

This approach to bundling/unbundling decisions applies to nearly all industries and especially to situations where the marginal costs are low and the customers' perceived value is rather high. Despite our earlier proviso that there are no hard-and-fast rules on bundling, we can offer some guidance that can serve as a rule of thumb: if a small number of customers see tremendous value in a certain feature, it makes little sense to offer that feature for free in order to make it available to a broader customer base. It makes much more sense to have this small customer segment pay the price it is willing to pay anyway.

Deciding whether to include a fee in your overall price or charge separately is only one small area of bundling. More difficult challenges arise when you must decide whether to bundle products that are comparable or complementary. Once you have a view of each segment's willingness to pay for the products you may want to bundle, you have a good basis for making decisions on whether to bundle.

Take the example of Rolling Stones and Fleetwood Mac concert tickets in figure 6-1. As we mentioned in chapter 3, many Rolling Stones fans would pay much more than face value to see the band perform live. This means they have excess willingness to pay for the ticket. But in our hypothetical example here, they are reluctant to pay full price for a ticket to see Fleetwood Mac, even though they are interested in the band. This is the middle situation in the figure. If a concert promoter offered a package of Stones and Fleetwood Mac tickets, that package would apply some of the excess willingness to pay for the Stones ticket to the Fleetwood Mac ticket. Many customers would buy the package and attend both concerts. Without the bundle, they would have only purchased the Stones ticket.

This only works when a customer has a reasonable willingness to pay for both parts of the bundle. If the promoter packaged the Stones with, say, Cher, the bundle discount would have to be extremely high or the package would probably flop. This is the example on the right

FIGURE 6-1

Bundling is an attractive option when preference for the individual products is significant, but not equal.

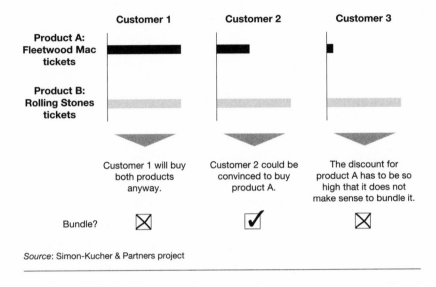

Source: Simon-Kucher & Partners project

in figure 6-1. The segments to which these artists appeal strongly would not have sufficient willingness to pay for the other ticket.

Concert tickets offer a relatively simple example. The more segments you have and the more products and services you have, however, the more critical it is that you understand the customers' underlying willingness to pay before you put bundles together.

Banks throughout the world find themselves facing this challenge. The repeal of the Glass-Steagall Act, which once mandated separation of banks, insurance companies, and insurance firms, has freed American banks to become more like their European cousins, which have long been allowed to offer banking, investment, and insurance services under one roof. The case of Bank42 Corporation, a leading European bank, illustrates both the complexity of the bundling task and the importance of understanding willingness to pay.[7]

Issue: Find the Optimal Product and Service Bundle

Company: Bank42 Corporation
Product: Checking accounts and credit cards
Source: Simon-Kucher & Partners project

A leading financial institution for decades, Bank42 Corporation now faces a confluence of new dynamics in retail banking, one of its core businesses. A new generation of sophisticated, computer-savvy customers enjoys much greater market transparency than their parents or grandparents could have imagined. The twenty-first-century banking customer can shop around quickly for the best deal, or forsake traditional banks entirely and shift business online.

The worst case for the banks, though, arises when the customers spread their business across several financial institutions in order to get the best possible deals from each of them. This causes problems for banks that have tried to compete by pushing attractive products such as free checking as a loss leader. This strategy is profitable only if it triggers cross-selling effects—that is, the customers who sign up for free checking use that bank's other retail banking services. If customers go elsewhere for their other banking needs, the strategy backfires.

When the managers of Bank42 took a hard look at their rising customer turnover (or "churn") and their declining profits, they saw all the ingredients for a loud, long strategic backfire if they did not intervene quickly. They decided to explore bundling as a potential solution. On paper the idea seemed to offer four advantages as a way to retain customers, attract new ones, and increase profits. First, it could attract customers by offering simplicity. Even though the individual products in the bundle might not always represent the best deal on the market, the whole package together could. Second, it would create exit barriers for customers. If customers decided to stop using the bundle of services, they would sever many relationships all at once (checking, credit card, debit card, etc.), all of which would need to be replaced. Third, it would create entry barriers for competition. The more comprehensive your attractive offering is, the more difficult it is for specialized competitors to lure customers away. Finally and most simply, the managers felt a properly designed bundle of services would allow them to sell more higher-margin services to customers who find such offers attractive.

To move from the paper solution to the practical one, the managers needed to understand the nuts and bolts of bundling. Bundles succeed when they transfer a customer's excess willingness to pay from one product to another, thus allowing a company to sell more of its products or services. The simple table in figure 6-2 shows how this could work in Bank42's case. The table shows the maximum amount that customers in two equally large groups ("emerging" and "traditional") would be willing to pay for online banking functionality and credit card use. You can see that each segment has a vastly different willingness to pay for each of the services, but the *sum* of their willingness to pay is roughly the same. Bank42 could take advantage

---

FIGURE 6-2

Bundling in banking

Customer segment	Maximum willingness to pay (in euros per month)		
	Online banking	Credit card	Sum for both services together
Emerging	5	0.50	5.50
Traditional	2	4	6.00

Source: Simon-Kucher & Partners

---

of this by bundling the two services at $5.50 (total sales = $11), rather than charging $5 for online banking and $4 for credit card use (total sales = $9).

The actual situation at Bank42 was much more complicated. Like most full-service retail banks, Bank42 offered checking and savings accounts, credit cards, fixed-rate investments, money market funds, personal loans, and mortgages.

You could even regard the simple checking account as a bundle of products and services. It includes account management, use of ATMs, and bank transfers. Most banks now charge one rate for these services (assuming they charge at all) instead of charging separately for account management and for each transaction. This is where Bank42 began its search for an attractive bundle. What could it add to its basic product—the traditional checking account—in order to retain customers, attract new ones, and increase profits? And how much should it charge?

To answer these questions, Bank42 employed many of the methods described in chapters 4 and 5. The number of possible bundle combinations seemed nearly infinite, which meant the project team quickly needed to narrow down the range of possibilities. An analysis of internal data and expert judgment from senior managers yielded two outcomes: an assessment of where Bank42's products stood relative to the competition, and a manageable list of elements to include in the bundle. Bank42 decided to look beyond the obvious and include nonbanking services like travel insurance in the selection process for bundle elements. To gain some validation of the competitive assessment and further narrow the list of bundles, the bank conducted focus groups in three critical regions.

The nonfinancial bundle elements fared surprisingly well and made the cut for the final round. Armed with this "short list" of bundle elements, Bank42 could now undertake more advanced research with customers to determine their willingness to pay. As we explained in chapter 5, the best way to determine willingness to pay is

FIGURE 6-3

Bank42's bundle offerings

	Standard	Comfort	Exclusive
Price per month (in euros)	5	8	11
Checking account management	X	X	X
Online banking	X	X	X
Debit card	X	X	X
Interest for checking account		X	X
Credit card		X	
Personal accident insurance for public transportation		X	
Gold credit card			X
Travel health insurance			X
Car insurance (abroad)			X
Travel cancellation expenses insurance			X
Travel service hotline			X

Source: Simon-Kucher & Partners

to include an indirect survey method, either discrete choice modeling (DCM) or adaptive conjoint analysis (ACA). In this case, ACA made more sense, because the company needed to understand the willingness to pay for each separate *element* of a potential bundle. DCM would have made more sense if the bank already had a clearer picture of what bundles might make sense, what elements they would comprise, and what bundles they would compete against directly.

The results of the survey allowed Bank42 to build a much more intricate version of the table shown in figure 6-2. This in turn enabled the bank to develop not one but three bundles, according to customers' willingness to pay for the underlying elements. Figure 6-3 shows these three bundles and what they comprise. Bank42's managers felt confident enough in the results that they decided to roll out the bundles nationally instead of conducting further tests.

By launching the three packages, Bank42 accomplished its goals of reducing customer turnover and improving profits. In the first year after the introduction, the bank's profits rose by 15 percent.

The Bonviva package offered by Credit Suisse is another example of a financial services bundle combining banking, insurance, and non-banking services. The bank makes the package available to customers who maintain a minimum balance of $20,000 or a minimum mortgage of $160,000. Bonviva includes a free checking account, a 50 percent reduction in credit card fees in the first year, a free debit card, more favorable interest rates, and commission-free traveler's checks. But it also includes emergency services (e.g., lost-key services), a lifestyle magazine with special offers for events and travel opportunities, as well as a range of discounts on hotels, car rentals, and restaurants.

Promote Your Products Heavily If You Know the Real Impact

How much financial benefit do companies really receive from their expenditures on advertising and promotion? The question is as old as advertising itself. In his book *Scientific Advertising*, originally published back in 1923, advertising pioneer Claude C. Hopkins denigrated the market expansion activities of one company by saying that "the object is commendable, but altruistic. The new business he creates is shared by his rivals. He is wondering why his sales increase is in no way commensurate with his expenditure."[8] When misdirected or improperly timed, promotional efforts amount to charitable contributions to your competitors.

When one of our clients launched a new medical treatment for respiratory conditions, it asked for guidance on whether it should invest in market expansion activities in the first twelve months after launch. As in most markets with an intermediary (in this case, the prescribing physician), the company would need to balance its investments in "push" and "pull" marketing. It would seem to make sense in theory for a company to invest heavily in both areas, especially for a new product. More "push" promotion from the sales force would encourage doctors to prescribe the drug more frequently, and more "pull" would prompt more patients to consult their doctors about having their condition treated.

Just as compelling, though, is the theory that there is an optimal way to balance both the timing and the amount of investment in the push and pull activities. Spend nothing or spend at the wrong time, and you cannot realistically expect an increase in sales. Spend large sums, and the law of diminishing returns sets in. You would probably fall into the trap Hopkins described earlier, in that you do your competitors a favor by building their sales at your expense. The answer, then, must lie somewhere in between.

This theoretical tug-of-war may lack the tension of the situation Bedrock Entertainment faced in chapter 5, but it met its resolution in a similar fashion. The client asked for additional evidence from the market. We decided to examine the promotional spending, sales, and market share data for other prescription drugs, and draw conclusions on what worked, what didn't, and what the company should do with its promotional dollars.

The market expansion activities behind these blockbusters all followed a similar pattern. They began by focusing on the push side in order to penetrate the market, attract share from existing competitors, and establish a clear point of differentiation. Scott A. Neslin of the Tuck School of Business at Dartmouth revealed that every dollar invested in direct sales activities aimed at the physician yielded a return of $10.29 in the first three years for blockbuster drugs launched between 1997 and 1999, nearly twice as much as the return from medical journal advertising.[9] It makes sense to emphasize push activities at this stage.

The risk comes when you enter the second phase, which is market expansion. You attempt to increase the number of patients treated in your class of prescription drugs. The makers of popular cholesterol-lowering agents such as Zocor and Lipitor have invested heavily in market expansion by ramping up the pull side with direct-to-customer advertising. Direct-to-customer advertisements by Imitrex, the pioneer migraine remedy marketed by Glaxo-SmithKline, offer a brief quiz to help potential patients distinguish between "normal" headaches and migraines.

This kind of differentiation is the critical point. As Hopkins indicated, you will always have free riders when you invest in market expansion activities—that is, your competitors will benefit to some degree. The sharper your point of differentiation, though, the more you can minimize the amount of business you create for competitors.

The antidepressant drug Paxil did not have a clear distinguishing message when its manufacturer attempted to increase market share in the crowded market for a class of drugs called selective serotonin reuptake inhibitors (SSRIs). These drugs help regulate the brain's level of the hormone serotonin, which is responsible for moods and emotions. Our regression analysis of market data showed that the company earned only ninety cents for every dollar spent on direct-to-customer advertising for Paxil. The push campaign succeeded in growing the market, but did not bring Paxil the share gains to justify the investment.

Pharmaceutical companies' investment in direct-to-customer advertising tends to peak three to four years after launch, before falling off significantly. The benchmark analysis showed that pharmaceutical companies put their advertising dollars to best use when they focus on push marketing until they have established a foothold and a clear point of differentiation. At that point, the balance shifts strongly toward pull marketing. The greater your point of differentiation, the lower the chances that your competitors will benefit more than you will from your market expansion activities.

While the precise timing of the shift from push to pull may differ by industry, this question is worth exploring when an intermediary wields a very strong influence on the end customers' product choice. These intermediaries include value-added resellers, insurance agents, investment advisors, or car dealers with multiple brands on their lots.

Summary

The key to finding and retrieving hidden profit is to make subtle changes to your marketing mix in order to wield its full power. Most companies in mature markets have room for improvement in how they segment their customers; select the products, services, and bundles they offer; and spend money on promotions.

The traditional basis for segmenting customers is how much they buy (volume) and where they operate (region). This shortcut is obsolete in most cases because managers now have much more data and analytical power available. A more profitable basis for segmenting customers is by preference and, especially, willingness to pay.

Once you have a clear and objective understanding of preferences and willingness to pay, you can make better decisions about what products and services to offer and how to bundle them. In some cases, unbundling is a wise strategy, because a high willingness to pay allows you to earn money. In other cases, consumer research can help you understand what to include in a bundle and how to price it in order to optimize your profit.

The greatest risk in spending on promotions is that you help your competitors more than you help yourself. Timing and focus make the difference. Your money is best spent when you can direct a specific segment of customers (and if appropriate, distributors) to your product rather than encouraging increased buying activity for the entire market.

Having the right segmentation, products, and promotion is essential. Price, however, is the most powerful element in the marketing mix. The next chapter explains how profit-oriented managers see price-value relationships differently from managers focused on market share, and how they can therefore raise prices profitably.

CHAPTER 7

Raise Your Prices to Get
the Profit You Deserve

Low prices and high profits rarely come together.
—Peter Drucker[1]

R AISING PRICES—and when, how, by how much, and why—
is one of the most important decisions a manager in a mature
market must make. It is also one of the most complicated and riski-
est. That might not seem so at first glance, because managers can
change prices instantly and frequently, at little or no expense. Airlines change their prices several times a day.

This enormous flexibility makes managers prone to abuse pricing. Of all the elements of the classic marketing mix, price is the
most flexible in the short term and the most potent. This makes it
the weapon of choice for managers steeped in a culture of aggression
or acquiescence. Think again of Dell's price war in the personal computer market, which we cited in chapter 2. Price actions cut Dell's
profits by an estimated $2 billion and turned the industry into a
"profit wasteland."[2] That is the destructive side of marketing.

Understand the Implications of Price Increases

Exploring the other side of marketing, the constructive side, begins with understanding the link between the value or performance you deliver and the prices you can charge. Price is the mirror of value. It is your instrument for extracting value from customers. Figure 7-1 shows how to plot these two aspects. You will notice a diagonal stripe that we refer to as a *consistency corridor*. If you plot the price of the products in a market against their perceived value in the eyes of the customers, they should ideally settle into this corridor.

Companies with hidden profit potential often find their products and services far below the consistency corridor. Think of Peninsula Auto Alloys in chapter 3, which felt its customers took it for granted and therefore did not demand prices that reflected the true

FIGURE 7-1

Profit-building actions companies can take involving value and price

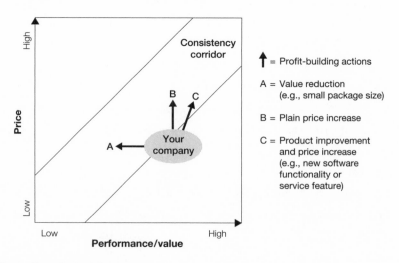

Source: Simon-Kucher & Partners

value it delivered. Kleber Enterprises in chapter 5 learned how it could move into the corridor after conducting hypothesis-driven research with its customers. Kinston moved into the corridor in chapter 5 by learning when it should offer more restrictive discounts, which is essentially a price increase.

But not every product lies underneath. Cortez in chapter 4 used the expert judgment tool to find out that it actually rested squarely within the consistency corridor and should forsake any price changes that would move it outside it.

In figure 7-1 you can see three useful means by which companies can raise their prices. A price increase can involve much more than simply raising prices by x percent. You can increase prices by offering less value at the same price. This decision is marked with "A" in figure 7-1. Think of grocery manufacturers who reduce package sizes without reducing prices. You can raise prices directly without changing how you serve your customer or what you offer them. That would be the decision marked with "B." Or you can provide your customers with additional value and charge an appropriate amount for it. That would represent "C."

Price-aggressive companies consciously and deliberately make marketing moves in the opposite direction. They attack by offering customers more value for the same price or the same value at lower prices. Technology companies make such moves frequently by adding more value to their products but charging lower prices. Sony, Nintendo, and Microsoft often make moves of this kind as they jockey for advantage in the market for video game consoles.

We devote the bulk of this chapter to showing you how companies have taken the actions shown in figure 7-1. In particular, we present examples of pure price increases and price increases based on added value (through product improvements or better service). Chapter 8 shows several examples of marketing's destructive power and how you can avoid making those destructive decisions.

When the companies in this chapter raised their prices, they combined the techniques from the first six chapters—fresh, fact-based assumptions, an appreciation of price response, analysis of internal data, hypothesis-driven research with customers, and preference-based segmentations—to give themselves the courage and confidence to raise prices when conventional wisdom would have suggested otherwise. The cases include not only an industrial supplier, but also a popular Internet service provider (ISP) and a Major League Baseball team.

Raise Prices If You Can Offer a Better Value Proposition

First, we focus on a company that used hypothesis-driven research to figure out how to change its pricing structure and capture a large amount of additional profit. This company made a "C" decision in figure 7-1. It learned how to provide customers with additional value and then extract it through higher prices and a different price structure.

CASE STUDY

Issue: Extract More Value Through Higher Prices

Company: Pluspumps
Product: Specialized pumps
Source: Simon-Kucher & Partners project

In many industries, from software to durable industrial goods, managers assess the value of what they buy by examining life-cycle cost or total cost of ownership (TCO). As you might expect, at least one competitor in those markets will try to differentiate itself by promising the lowest TCO. The competitor defends the up-front cost of purchasing its products by stressing the product's longevity, low maintenance and operating costs, or high resale value. This kind of pricing approach works if the TCO is truly a very important issue to the customers. Only then does it make sense to defend a high price with a comparatively lower TCO. Just because the logic works for many investment goods, however, does not mean that the customers of other products will automatically embrace it.

That is the lesson that customers taught Pluspumps, which sells specialized pumps for viscous materials.[3] Wear and tear of this hard work limits the lifetime of the pump. Pluspumps' management stressed the value of its products and based its prices on life-cycle cost. They elevated their sales pitch to a fine art by taking purchase price, operating costs, maintenance, spare parts, and product lifetime into account.

When we started to investigate where they might have unexplored profit potential, we challenged management with a heretical hypothesis: maybe customers don't buy pumps because of their life-cycle costs. In other words, maybe customers don't bother with the detailed cost-driven analysis of which Pluspumps was so proud.

In-depth interviews with customers verified this hypothesis. Out of ten important factors in the customers' decision to buy a pump, life-cycle costs ranked next to last. The number one factor was reliability, followed by the availability of spare parts. The customers' rationale for these rankings made sense. The investment in a pump was minuscule compared with the investment in the entire plant, but the pumps' reliability was critical. The failure of just one pump could cause the shutdown of an entire plant. The resulting lost production would cost the company far more than the pumps themselves. While life-cycle costs were nice to know, they hardly played a role in the purchase decision.

Because of this information, Pluspumps stopped basing price quotes on its treasure trove of cost information. Instead, it raised the purchase price significantly, but made a range of spare parts available to customers on-site. This guaranteed immediate availability and would help customers reduce or prevent downtime should a pump fail. Pluspumps' costs rose by around 5 percent, but transaction prices rose by 10 percent with no loss in volume. The team had found a way to achieve higher prices and give customers a better deal at the same time. The entire process, including retraining of the sales force and the release of new communication materials, took less than six months to accomplish.

Pluspumps had taken a timely second look at a product whose value proposition in the marketplace seemed obvious to the company. What it learned helped it to retool itself rather than its product. It achieved higher revenue per transaction without tightening or replacing a single screw on the physical product. Instead, it captured its incremental profit by catching up to its customers' way of thinking.

Raise Prices to Preserve Profits in a Declining Market

Think of one of your products or services that faces increasing competition. Quick question: are the prices for that product or service too high? Most managers would answer yes, particularly for products in a declining market. One of three events usually triggers such a decline: a competitor may have felt that the profit pool in your market is so vast that it wants to seize a share for itself, either by eroding one of your competitive advantages or by accepting less profit than you do; a company may have developed a technology that makes your product obsolete, as the word processor did to the typewriter; or in rare cases, a company succeeds in producing comparable goods or services at substantially and more sustainable lower costs.

Regardless of circumstances, your product or service has peaked. You now face what is most likely the last critical crossroads in that product's life cycle. How should you cope with this decline? Would lower prices revitalize the business by fighting the competition and keeping your volume at a high level? Gut feeling and conventional wisdom would recommend price cuts. We suggest an alternative when you have a product that seems doomed to slow growth, decline, or even obsolescence: keep prices steady or even raise them, rather than cutting them in an effort to maintain or increase volume. Steady or higher prices will allow you to harvest the greatest possible amount of profit from that business.

To make that decision, you need to think through the consequences at two levels. You want to make the best decision right now, but you want to avoid doing something that could actually accelerate the decline of your business or limit your leeway to make decisions in the months ahead. You also need to know exactly where you rest on the profit curve in figure 3-1 (see chapter 3). Lower prices can indeed yield higher profits for you, but if and only if current prices are higher than the price that would give you your peak profit level. This worked for Kent Molding at one of its customers (see chapter 4), but Kent's situation is an exception to the rule. Most companies' prices are simply too low, even when the industry is declining and the temptation is great to scorch the earth and exit the business quickly.

America Online (AOL) refused to scorch the earth in its dial-up Internet business. We estimate that its decision to raise prices netted the company an extra $70 million in incremental profit in a market headed for a sharp decline.

Issue: How Much to Change Prices in Anticipation of Market Decline

Company: America Online
Product: Dial-up Internet service
Source: Analysis of publicly available
information and interviews
with market experts

We wholeheartedly praise the AOL management team for two decisions they took in 2001, as the market for dial-up Internet service showed signs of peaking.[4] First, they not only eschewed price cuts, they actually raised their prices despite clear competitive threats. Second, they artfully communicated their intentions to the market ahead of their actual decision. We address the first point now, and the second in chapter 10.

In early 2001, the newly merged AOL Time Warner found itself in a market share battle for dial-up Internet service. While Microsoft's MSN had become more aggressive in its marketing, EarthLink spoofed AOL mercilessly in its television ads. NetZero entered the market at less than half of AOL's price per month. To make matters worse, a technological threat loomed: broadband.

What should AOL have done? The knee-jerk response called for them to slash prices to protect the business. In the end, AOL ignored conventional wisdom and actually raised its price in May 2001 from $21.95 per month to $23.90 per month. To understand AOL's motivation and what the price change meant, we discovered that four factors had played a role:

- AOL knew it had high switching barriers because its clientele—convinced of the "So easy to use, no wonder it's number one" tagline—would be reluctant to go elsewhere. Switchers would lose their e-mail addresses and buddy lists. Starting anew just wouldn't be worth the hassle.

- AOL knew subscriber growth would soon slow down. It had around 23 million subscribers, nearly four times as many as MSN, which was watching AOL's every move. If growth slowed, attracting new subscribers with a lower price would become less relevant, and increasing average revenue per user more relevant.

- AOL's costs had risen significantly, as its subscribers enjoyed the benefits of the flat-rate service. Because it had always maintained a fixed margin on dial-up (essentially a cost-plus strategy), AOL would need a higher price to restore balance—that is, to preserve its fixed margin.[5]

- AOL knew that broadband would ultimately destroy its dial-up business. The price increase marked the first conscious move toward an exit strategy. When the company unveiled its broadband strategy, its domestic subscriber base had already fallen by 13 percent to around 20 million. But in the fifteen-month period between the price increase and the broadband announcement, the company had collected an extra $1.95 every month from these remaining 20 millions subscribers.

Granted, AOL no longer collected money each month from the 3 million subscribers it had gradually lost. But if you compare the actual results with a "do nothing" scenario, you will see that AOL had improved its situation by raising prices. It generated between $70 million and $100 million in extra revenues, if one assumes that half of the customers that left AOL did so because of broadband. Because the mere act of increasing prices created essentially no extra costs, most of that revenue flowed straight to the bottom line as pure profit. Our estimates are also conservative, because AOL's subscriber base actually continued to grow strongly for several months, even after the price increase, before starting its anticipated decline.

By thinking through the consequences and examining its options, AOL found a counterintuitive and profitable way to manage its decline. It resisted the temptation to go thrill seeking with some heroic plan to fight for market share and "rescue" the dial-up business.

Increase Prices for Selected Customer Segments

How should a company increase prices for specific segments, especially when customers' involvement in the product is very high? Let's add a further twist to this question and say that the media will scrutinize every price change you make as well as the rationale behind it. Because this constellation occurs frequently in sports, we will describe the process the Toronto Blue Jays baseball team used to set its single-game prices for the 2004 season.

The Blue Jays' situation is more complicated than AOL's or Pluspumps' because the team offers seats in many different price categories. Each of these categories corresponds to a different level of value, depending, for example, on how close the seat is to the action. Thus, the Blue Jays have price-value points all over figure 7-1. The team needed to know which ones lay within the consistency corridor, which ones lay outside it, and what changes it needed to make to bring them all into a consistent corridor.

CASE STUDY

Issue: Set Single-game Ticket Prices

Company: Toronto Blue Jays Baseball Club
Product: Major league baseball tickets
Source: Simon-Kucher & Partners project

The ubiquity of sports, the allure of luxury boxes in new stadiums, and the salaries players earn conspire to reinforce the impression that sports is big business. The Toronto Blue Jays, a Major League Baseball team, are no exception. Owned by Rogers Communications, Canada's leading communications company, they play at the Rogers Centre (formerly known as SkyDome), the first-ever stadium with a retractable roof. They signed one player, award-winning pitcher Roy Halladay, to a contract extension that will pay him $42 million over four years.[6] Despite these trappings, however, baseball more resembles a collection of small, family-run businesses than one monolithic "big business."

"The industry definitely needs to get more sophisticated," said Steve Smith, the former vice president of ticket sales for the Blue Jays. "Even today baseball still resembles the old days when all clubs were essentially small businesses."[7]

The key question is where that sophistication should begin. Few other businesses in the world lend themselves to quantification as easily as baseball. Teams such as the Oakland A's, Boston Red Sox, and the Blue Jays themselves have very elaborate quantitative systems for evaluating players and how much they should pay them.

No club, however, has a similarly advanced infrastructure to figure out how much fans should pay either for individual games or for season-ticket packages, which account for one-third to two-thirds of a club's entire revenue. The irony is that they have the right status data available, such as how much people paid to sit in what seat for what game. They simply needed to use that status data to generate response data, much as Casual Male did with its historical data in the case in chapter 4. As sports business columnist Vicki L. James said, the answer for how to make the business more data driven "lies outside of the traditional sports approach and within the strategies that have proven successful in other industries."[8]

Traditionally, sports teams charge the same price for a particular seat for every game. Following the lead of other teams in professional and college sports, the Blue Jays introduced *variable pricing*. Variable pricing means that tickets to some games are more expensive or less expensive depending on when the game is played and who the opponent is. The experience of other teams with whether variable pricing generated higher profits was inconclusive. Outside of anecdotal evidence, no one knew for sure whether it helped or harmed a team's revenue and profit.

As the Blue Jays evaluated their own variable-pricing scheme and decided whether to retain it for the following season, both opponents and proponents emerged. Just as in the Bedrock case (see chapter 5), both sides had loads of arguments they could present eloquently. The opponents of the system felt that variable pricing confused fans. They doubted that it made any notable financial difference. Proponents argued that the differentiation helped boost revenue because it matched better with willingness to pay.

The Blue Jays front office was united in the belief that the club could find opportunities to generate more revenue. But it was unsure whether variable pricing had fulfilled its potential. The monkey wrench in the debate, as usual, was the industry's conventional wisdom, which claimed that on-field performance explains 80 percent of attendance. No one at the Blue Jays, however, had yet exposed this wisdom to a rigorous test.

To settle the issue, the proponents took on the burden of proof. We helped them build a model based on multivariate regression analysis that could predict attendance at a particular set of games and could also isolate what factors influenced attendance in each section of the Rogers Centre. The Blue Jays put their status data to work in order to generate response data and then build what-if scenarios to determine which set of prices would generate the highest revenue. (Because we consider the marginal cost of a ticket sale to be negligible, the increase in revenue would equate to the Blue Jays' increase in profit.)

To assemble the raw data, we created a data framework by combining information from separate, independently maintained databases. The resulting collection comprised over 5 million data points, including the actual price paid for each seat at each game.

Because the Blue Jays offered numerous single-game promotional discounts throughout the season, the actual price paid for a ticket varied by seat and game, even when the face value did not. This rich source of real-life variance in prices allowed us to examine price response and price elasticity. In addition to ticket price, we included several other variables in the analysis, including opponent, day of week, month, souvenir giveaways (such as bobbleheads), the team's position in the standings, length of current winning or losing streak, and whether the Toronto Maple Leafs hockey team played that night.

Our two major findings were clear. First, only four variables had an overarching effect on attendance at the Rogers Centre: ticket price, day of the week, month, and opponent. Second, the impact of each variable differed greatly by section within their stadium—that is, by customer segment. No single factor influenced attendance equally across the entire stadium. The two measures of "winning"— position in the standings and length of current winning/losing streak—had a strong impact only in certain sections, and not to the same consistent degree as the four major factors cited earlier. Other variables, such as the Maple Leafs' schedule, likewise influenced attendance strongly in certain sections of the stadium but hardly at all in others. It appeared that each stadium section catered to a different customer segment with different preferences from the fans in neighboring sections.

Empowered by the availability of response data on a section-by-section basis, the team's management could now estimate the financial consequences of its decisions, and build what-if scenarios. Should they have more bargain nights or fewer? How much higher or lower should ticket prices be for certain opponents or on certain days of the week? How does attendance change as the gap between ticket prices in different seat categories widens or narrows?

The evidence also provided concrete support for certain hypotheses that club officials already had. Rob Godfrey, the team's senior vice president for communications and external relations, had strongly advocated that the club charge significantly less for certain seats in the SkyDeck, the ring of seats in the stadium's uppermost deck. The model not only confirmed his hunch, but also helped the Blue Jays decide just how far they could afford to reduce prices.

Figure 7-2 shows how the Blue Jays adjusted their ticket prices for "regular" games in 2004 versus 2003. Because of our recommendations, they increased prices for premium seats, in recognition of the factors that drive attendance at the Rogers Centre. For "premium" games, prices would be slightly higher than shown in figure 7-2 and slightly lower for "value" games. All figures are in Canadian dollars. Prices also rose slightly for some seats in the SkyDeck (the

FIGURE 7-2

Single-game ticket prices for the Toronto Blue Jays, before and after the price changes

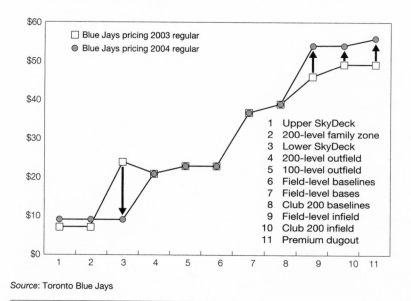

Source: Toronto Blue Jays

two data points on the left), but this change was more than offset by a drastic reduction in prices for other SkyDeck seats (the third data point from the left). For "value" games, prices for all seats in the Sky-Deck would be just $2.

One final constraint on any sports team's decision making is public acceptance, which depends on how the local press responds to the changes. In this case, the press responded positively to both the changes and the logic behind them. One columnist commented that "[m]ost of the new price increases come at the high end of the price chart, where an $8 jump isn't likely to rankle the Richie Riches. So strike this as a victory for the common folk."[9]

Smith and Godfrey had taken the Blue Jays' price-setting process to a more objective level. Armed with the model and with better insight into what drives attendance, the Blue Jays could now put numbers behind their assumptions. They could estimate how much certain decisions would cost them and what certain decisions would earn them.

Both the Blue Jays and Casual Male cases show what a company can accomplish and how fast change can take hold when a company subjects its decision making to a more rigorous, quantitative process. In the Blue Jays case, attendance and revenue increased in the first season after implementing the new pricing structure, even though the team finished the season with a worse win-loss record than the year before.

Use Price as an Indicator of Value
for a "Low Involvement" Product

How should companies capture extra profits when customers do not care about how much they pay, either because they lack the time to search for the best deal or because they need to buy the product urgently?

Admit it: at some point in your life you have watched the game show *The Price Is Right* and felt triumphant when a contestant couldn't figure out how much the microwave oven or the box of macaroni and cheese really cost, but you could. But when most of us step into a home improvement store, club store, or department store, we become that poor contestant.

In one week recently, the authors ventured out to buy a padlock, a snow shovel, paper plates, a sink faucet, and a fax machine. Each purchase was unplanned, prompted by either curiosity or a sudden need. None of us had any idea how much these things cost or ought to cost. Nor did we do any substantive research beforehand. But each of us left the store with the feeling that we got a good deal, maybe too good a deal. We will use the purchase of the padlock to show how the retailer may have passed up profit opportunities.

In hindsight we now know that you cannot just go to a home improvement store and expect to buy a padlock. Padlocks have many subspecies. You have several to choose from, ranging in price from $5 to $12. Unless you have some obscure piece of knowledge stashed away in your brain to give you an advantage, you would follow one of three paths:

- Buy the cheapest one, because there is nothing special about the padlock you need.

- Buy the most expensive one, in the belief that it's not that much money and the most expensive one must be the best.

- Buy the one priced somewhere in the middle, so that you have neither the lowest quality nor the highest price.

The author in question took the third path and bought one for $8. In doing so, he became an example of what is known as the *compromise effect*, under which brands or products gain market share when they form the in-between option in a set of alternatives.[10] But what if the range of price had been $8 to $12 instead of $5 to $12? He said he would have probably still bought the one priced in the middle, for the same reasons.

This phenomenon provides retailers with an opportunity to use price itself as an indicator of value. Irrationally or not, most people reflexively associate lower prices with lower quality and higher prices with higher quality. Unless they take a closer look to see if they are really receiving fair value for the money, they use that reflexive assessment as the basis for their purchase decision.

The truth is, the only reason anyone knows how much a padlock should cost is that leading retail outlets tell us how much. Within reason, they have considerable freedom in setting prices for products that individual customers buy infrequently. This fact alone means they can easily overlook potential for higher profits. Let's say for the sake of argument that The Home Depot marks up its padlocks by 100 percent. It procures the $8 padlock for $4. If it priced that padlock at $10 instead and narrowed the range so that this price point occupied the middle, it would earn 50 percent more per padlock. Profit would more than double on the $5 padlocks if you moved them to $8 to anchor the bottom end of the range.

Is that price gouging? In a state of emergency such as a natural disaster, charging higher prices may violate state laws and business ethics. But in the normal course of business, it certainly is not price gouging. Your sense that it might constitute price gouging derives from two things:

- The much lower anchor price we gave you at the beginning of this story, which fixed your frame of reference

- The deep-seated notion that the final price of a product should somehow be linked directly to its costs

But are you privy to The Home Depot's cost structure, or Lowe's? We'd be surprised if you were. Unless you work for a lock manufacturer or write for *Inside Self-Storage* magazine (yes, it exists), you probably haven't the faintest idea about the wholesale price of a padlock, and in your moment of need you still don't give it much thought.

These amounts sound trivial, but across large portfolios they can accrue very quickly. They represent a rich source of potential profit. To the typical consumer, a home improvement store is little more than a vast collection of low-involvement products. To a hobbyist or heavy user, the store looks much different. Introducing a more complex pricing structure could help keep these two very distinct segments separate. The store could charge a high up-front fee in exchange for substantial discounts on certain ranges of products in the store. The heavy users would take advantage of this offer and receive the lower prices day to day. But unless home improvement or gardening were your main hobby, you would never take advantage of that offer. You would be free to choose either option, but you would probably pay the higher off-the-shelf prices for your padlocks, snow shovels, and sink faucets. And we'd bet that you would never even be aware that the person standing behind you in line would pay less at checkout for the same sink faucet.

Be Careful Changing Prices When Your Costs Change

When companies in mature markets see a sharp rise in their raw material costs, they often fall back on another shortcut based on conventional wisdom. They pass most or all of the cost increase on to customers through higher prices. Their math is simple. If your costs rise by 5 percent, you should raise prices by the same amount and use the higher costs as the justification. Costs in this case can include not only raw materials and energy costs, but also exchange-rate fluctuations.

As with all of the other corporate shortcuts we've discussed in this book, this one has a quantitative nature and some basis in fact.

But it also has the dangerous potential to mislead managers and cause them to sacrifice profit they deserve. To understand how this works, think back to the profit curve in figure 3-1. If your variable costs have risen significantly, the optimal price you can charge—that is, the price that gives you your peak profit performance—may indeed move to the right. How far to the right it moves depends on the price elasticity and the magnitude of the change in costs. But it is rarely advisable to raise prices by the same percentage your costs have increased. Doing so will cost you money. For most realistic cases, it is correct to say that price changes should be smaller than cost changes.

The same dynamic applies to situations when your variable costs decrease significantly. In that case, your profit curve might shift to the left. The price at which you earn the greatest profit would then be lower. But again, the change may be very slight. This latter phenomenon explains why companies with a very large cost advantage, such as Dell or Southwest Airlines, remain profitable even though they charge prices that are much lower than their competitors'.

Again, we stress that the world Dell and Southwest created for themselves is unattainable for most companies in mature markets. Most competitors in those markets have a similar cost basis and experience similar effects when raw materials costs rise or fall. Trying to use a marginally lower cost basis as an argument for price cutting or aggressive behavior is a surefire way to put your profits at risk, as is the idea of passing along productivity improvements to your customers in full.

Keep in mind one final point on reflecting cost changes in your prices. If your fixed costs rise or fall, the change has absolutely no effect on where your profit-optimal price is. The summit remains where it is. The locations of the peaks and valleys of your profit curve are determined only by customer willingness to pay and your variable costs. Fixed costs do not matter in this calculation.

Remember the Price-Value Consistency Corridor When Negotiating Prices

Not every company goes to the market with one main price, like America Online, or around a dozen price points, as the Toronto Blue Jays do. Industrial suppliers, for example, negotiate hundreds or even thousands of prices in individual transactions over the course of a year. The circumstances of these transactions—customer, product spec, service requirements, application, volume required, and terms of the agreement—make it very hard to compare one transaction with the next.

Nonetheless, companies that negotiate prices with their customers can still benefit from the price-value corridor shown in figure 7-1. It forms the final piece of the puzzle we have assembled in the previous six chapters. We explain the role it plays as we close this chapter with advice on how to push through higher prices in a negotiation, or at least hold the ground on prices.

- *Force the customer into trading value for price.* The customer always has the upper hand in the negotiation if you spend most of your time talking about price levels. But providing them with a direct concession is the equivalent of a price cut. The counter-move required is to offer a lower price only if the total value you offered is reduced as well. Figure 7-3 illustrates this. The reduction in value could take many forms, ranging from less technical service, a shorter warranty period, slower delivery, or a lower-quality product spec.

- *Use the value of each product aspect to your advantage.* We advise companies in mature markets that even though they might sell "commodity" products, they hardly ever compete in a commodity business. In other words, the products you make

FIGURE 7-3

Downscaling allows you to preserve profit. Accommodate a customer's request for a lower price, but offer that customer less overall value.

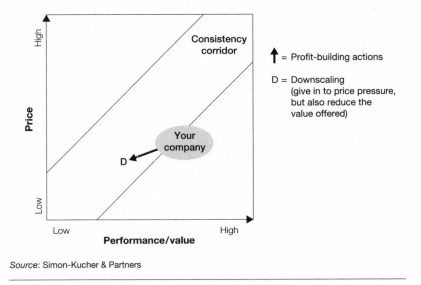

Source: Simon-Kucher & Partners

might indeed be functionally interchangeable with most of those your competitors offer. But you aren't selling wheat or gold. Who you are, how you sell, and how you support your product often make all the difference between closing the sale and losing it. These factors—whether tangible or intangible—often trump price in importance. (Of course, no savvy buyer would ever admit this in your presence!) The amount of time and resources your customer willingly commits to the negotiation process is often a signal of how valuable those additional aspects are. While this information may not always enable you to charge higher prices, it certainly gives you the confidence to hold the line and avoid making unnecessary concessions.

- *Remember that sometimes concessions are necessary.* A price negotiation is never solely about the product and the price. At the end of the day, it is a discussion among people, each with their own motivations and incentives. Your opponent in the negotiation may need a victory because he or she is rewarded for the concessions extracted from suppliers. Be prepared to have some items you can concede in order to accommodate your opponent. But also be prepared to walk away if the customer clearly refuses to accept an appropriate price for the value you deliver.

Price increases are complex to plan and execute. As we mentioned in our example near the end of chapter 1, no other action you undertake will integrate the various lessons, tools, and techniques in this book in the way that a price increase does. It offers you your greatest opportunity to earn higher profits. You cannot make the decision lightly.

Summary

Price increases represent a substantial source of profit. You need to make sure, however, that you understand the implications of the price changes before you raise prices.

The form and magnitude of the price increase will depend on your location on the price-value map shown in figure 7-1. Although it sounds counterintuitive, raising prices is usually the most profitable strategy to maintain or increase profits when your market starts to decline. You can raise prices directly without adding value. You can hold prices constant but reduce the value delivered. You can increase prices after enhancing your value proposition through quality improvements or additional services.

Several other facts can help you determine whether and how much to raise prices.

- When customers have a low level of involvement with your product, price is often their primary indicator of value. Use this to your advantage.

- Never assume that you can pass on higher raw materials costs to your customers in full. Your profit-optimal price does indeed change, but the magnitude depends on price elasticity, not just the change in variable costs.

- Fixed costs play no role in finding the optimal price point for a product—that is, the price that puts you at the summit in figure 3-1.

Many companies, especially business-to-business ones, negotiate prices individually rather than setting them publicly. Price negotiations should always be a give-and-take between value and price, not simply a question of "how much." If you negotiate prices, remember that your opponent often needs a victory. Be prepared to make concessions where it hurts least—that is, somewhere besides price.

Finally, the price-value relationship also has a destructive side. The next chapter explains how you can recognize and avoid it.

CHAPTER 8

Don't Ingratiate Yourself
with Customers

An analysis that prevents you from taking a certain course of action
can sometimes be more valuable than a revolutionary idea.

—John D. C. Little, professor,
MIT Sloan School of Management[1]

PETER DRUCKER once said that "marketing means seeing the whole business through the eyes of the customer."[2] In one sense, the authors could not agree more. In each chapter thus far, we have shown you how to place your focus on your customers in order to understand their preferences, their behavior, and their willingness to pay.

But some marketing and sales professionals take Drucker's statement too literally. They allow the maxim of delighting the customer to dictate every move they make, including the prices they charge. A marketing official once told us that he could not understand why his division lost money: "We have the highest levels of customer satisfaction in our industry. We offer great quality and service at low prices."

As you surely know by now, value delivered and value extracted are intimately related. If you make overdelivery the cornerstone of your marketing strategy, but you do not earn your fair share in return, you have put yourself on a slow path to financial ruin. Remember that your untapped profit potential, the difference between good performance and peak performance, lies in your customers' pockets. It represents the money they would willingly give you if you found the right way to extract it. How can you continue to defend any marketing approach that allows your customers to keep 1 to 3 percent of your annual revenue, which is the amount of incremental profit we cited in chapter 1?

Learn When to Sacrifice Customer Satisfaction in Favor of Profit

This chapter serves as a warning against what we referred to in chapter 7 as the destructive side of marketing. It demonstrates the folly of taking the aggressive actions shown in figure 8-1, which is the mirror image of figure 7-1. It provides more detail on the profit-destroying actions that aggressive and acquiescent companies undertake. They fall into three categories:

- *Customer giveaways.* These often amount to little more than literally giving customers something for nothing. Well-intended loyalty programs often stray down this path. The inevitable problem arises when customers start to view these giveaways as entitlements and develop an appetite for more. Profit destruction begins when companies start trying do outdo each other with their giveaways. This is the "E" arrow in figure 8-1.

- *Value attacks.* Companies need to have a thorough grasp of what their products and services are worth. Without it, they run the risk of losing money on the improvements they make to their products. Why should additional, meaningful customer

FIGURE 8-1

The dark side of marketing: these actions put your profit at considerable risk.

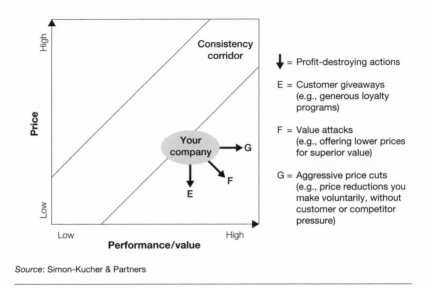

Source: Simon-Kucher & Partners

value result in lower prices? This is the arrow marked "F" in figure 8-1.

- *Aggressive price cuts.* The most baffling action of all is the surprise price cut. Companies in mature markets cannot win price wars unless they have an insurmountable advantage in terms of costs or product quality. Even if they "win" a price war, the evidence is not clear that these companies can ever recoup the profit they sacrificed in order to increase their volume and thus their market share. This is the arrow marked "G" in figure 8-1.

The next three sections use concrete examples to show how these actions threaten not just the companies' own profit, but yours as well.

Launch Loyalty Programs Only If Competitors Can't Copy Them

Imitation is the sincerest form of flattery, according to the seemingly innocuous cliché. It implies that the honor of being imitated could even be a worthwhile goal. That may ring true in private life, but it rings hollow in the business world, where imitation is the sincerest form of competitive threat.

Yes, a competitive threat may indeed be very flattering. However, we would expect that, given a choice, most managers and executives would prefer profitability to flattery anytime. Just ask the shareholders of Kmart, who have seen what has happened since Sam Walton copied their business model, right down to the basis for the store's name, some forty years ago.

The same logic explains the curse of loyalty programs, which have proliferated across industries and across the world over the last thirty years. The term *customer loyalty* has such a positive connotation that one automatically assumes it is desirable, even necessary, to foster it. But is this really true? And if so, is a formal loyalty program the wisest choice? Managers should not assume that a customer loyalty program would make their companies more profitable. Instead, they should understand the curse of loyalty programs: the ease with which competitors can imitate them.

Though it may involve some work, competitors can usually mimic a loyalty program quickly, much as they can match higher discounts or lower prices. What seemed at first like a nice point of differentiation becomes neutralized as competitors introduce similar or even better programs. That's when the vicious cycle begins, as companies rush to top a competitor's loyalty program only to see that same competitor pump up its program with yet more benefits.

Most loyalty programs are little more than price cuts paid out to customers in goods and services instead of cash. They intensify pressures in the market by creating another vicious circle, as competitors try to outdo each other. You should offer them only when you can sustain your differentiation because you offer customers a unique advantage. Competitors have failed to neutralize or undermine the advantage of loyalty programs only when the product or service itself formed the core of the "loyalty" program, or when the program itself offered a truly unique advantage. The former situation reflects the attachment people have to Apple computers, Harley-Davidson motorcycles, and Porsche cars. Their heavy users need no extra push to demonstrate their loyalty.[3] The case of the German Railroad Company's customer card illustrates the latter situation.

CASE STUDY

Issue: What Steps to Take to "Undo" an Unsuccessful Marketing Decision

Company: DB, or Deutsche Bahn (German Railroad Company)
Product: Loyalty card
Source: Simon-Kucher & Partners project

Done cleverly, a loyalty program can change the structure of how people pay, while offering an additional, "softer" benefit. Pinpointing exactly what that soft benefit is, however, can challenge even the managers of a successful program. The German Railroad Company had overlooked one of those soft factors in its discount card program and discovered it only after making an unfortunate change to its program.

The original card cost $140 per year and entitled customers to a 50 percent discount on all tickets purchased. More than 3 million people had purchased or renewed the discount card each year since its initial launch in 1994. This led the company and most observers to call the card a success. Then Deutsche Bahn came across a critique of the card. A book on pricing policy asserted that "the card has functioned only as a rebate instrument, with no emotional attachment. Its function as a means of customer retention is limited."[4] In 2002 Deutsche Bahn launched a new price system that replaced the old discount card with a new card with a reduced annual fee of $60 and just a 25 percent discount. In addition, it introduced individual tickets with discounts of up to 40 percent and airline-style conditions (prebooking, Saturday-night stay-overs, and restricted availability).

What ensued may rank as prominently in German business history as the launch of New Coke in 1985 does in the United States. In the first few months of 2003, the pricing system met its Waterloo. Customer protests raged, fanned by front-page stories in both the tabloid and the business press. Passengers also proved that while the company may effectively have a monopoly on the rails, it certainly has no monopoly on intercity transportation. They abandoned the trains. Sales collapsed.

The company needed to react. The default option—advocated by many pressure groups—would have been to restore the traditional card with the 50 percent discount. Coca-Cola had made a similar move when it relaunched its traditional formulation under the Classic brand name shortly after the reaction to New Coke became clear.

But the company first wanted to understand what went wrong. You might think that this was a classic case of a company going one step too far in curtailing customer incentives. However, old assumptions about how people perceived the 50 percent discount proved incorrect. A significant share of the old cardholders had not earned back their initial investment over the course of the year, because they did not travel often enough or far enough. Because of the up-front investment, the average rebate across all card customers was less than 30 percent. Absolute savings, then, could not explain the widespread appeal of the old card.

The card was much more than a means to offer a rebate. Business and leisure travelers alike appreciated the card's *convenience* in that it guaranteed the cardholder the best possible price no matter what. They never had to review the railroad's numerous and complicated array of special offers. The new discount level of 25 percent erased that benefit. It forced a return to the old days, when the buyers had to learn the head-scratching intricacies of the price system in order to find the best offer. After years of stability and certainty, travelers suddenly wondered whether they still had a good deal.

Travelers also enjoyed the flexibility of the original card. In contrast to the terms and conditions attached to most bargain transportation tickets, the old card had no restrictions or limitations. You had maximum flexibility. You could ride on any train, at any time, to any destination and still receive your rebate of 50 percent. You could buy your ticket weeks in advance, at the last minute, or even on the train itself after boarding and be confident that you had paid the lowest available price.

The German Railroad Company eventually relaunched the old card, but with a higher card price of $200 per year for second class and $400 for first class. The public and the media broadly welcomed the decision, despite the higher fee, and the card quickly made a spectacular comeback. After the first year on the market, it was clear that the new loyalty concept was a big success, in spite of a price some 50 percent higher than the original card's.

Don't Create Customer Entitlements

Customers adore loyalty programs and free customer cards. And why shouldn't they? As competition increases, their perks from these programs become entitlements in the truest sense of the word. They are extremely hard to take away. Like governments trying to reduce welfare and retirement benefits, companies face considerable resistance if they try to reduce or eliminate entitlements.

Granted, not all loyalty initiatives create expensive entitlements. The best initiatives allow a company to capture higher profits without a significant monetary investment and without mortgaging the future by carrying huge liabilities to customers. In 2003, Continental Airlines began offering the Elite Access program to passengers who pay the regular fare. The program puts customers on standby for an upgrade to first class and gives them priority boarding and priority treatment at the security screening. Make no mistake: Continental had to offer this new program in addition to its miles-based loyalty program. There was no way (at least in the beginning) for Continental to end something that had become an industry standard of customer entitlements.

For the business travelers who do not squeeze Continental's rates with corporate discounts or special tickets, this is a rare and highly prized incentive. The trick about this particular benefit is its pay-to-play character: customers need to pay full fare to earn an incentive that has almost no variable cost to Continental. Once the plane departs, the standby commitment ends. Continental has no further liability. Frequent-flier miles, however, accumulate. That is how they have become entitlements.

The *Economist* estimated that the world's second-largest currency in circulation behind the U.S. dollar is the frequent-flier mile.[5] CNN Money pegged the total volume in circulation at 9 trillion miles.[6] All these miles face a steep devaluation in the form of usage limitations, higher "prices" for premium products, changes in status privileges, or outright expirations. After dispersing trillions of miles to entice customers, the airlines now need to honor these commitments.

Yet because every airline has a loyalty program—from the legacy hub-and-spoke carriers to the small point-to-point start-ups—customers feel entitled to their miles and giveaways. The airline frequent-flier mile or free ticket has become a cost of doing business, not a customer incentive or "bonus." Curtailing these entitlements is not easy, as US Airways learned when it tried to cut customer loyalty entitlements in an effort to focus on "premium travelers." To achieve this focus, it would take benefits away from passengers who bought nonrefundable tickets. Miles earned on most of their flights would no longer count toward earning the preferred, gold, or silver status in the US Airways bonus program. Passengers could not use corporate discount programs for many nonrefundable fares, nor could they stand by for alternate flights.[7]

"Someone who flies a lot isn't necessarily loyal if what they're doing is buying the lowest-priced ticket every time they fly," explained Ben Baldanza, senior vice president at US Airways. "That's not necessarily the kind of loyalty we want to reward. We want to reward those people who pay a premium for the services we offer."[8]

This move had unexpected, almost paradoxical consequences: the "better" loyalty program actually caused many of the airline's rank-and-file business fliers to go on strike. These passengers felt they had paid their dues by acting as fiscally responsible corporate citizens and flying regularly with US Airways' nonrefundable fares. They considered the service reliable and reasonably priced. But with Mr. Baldanza's changes, they had lost their reward. These customers came together online, formed the Cockroach Club, and wore cockroach pins with the US Airways logo in order to express their displeasure over their treatment at the airline's hands.

The airline eventually relented and started to cooperate. At Roachfest 2004, the Cockroaches' annual gathering, US Airways senior vice president for corporate affairs Christopher L. Chiames joined the meeting to discuss issues facing the airline. "Sometimes the answer is no," Chiames told the meeting. "We can't give customers everything they want, but we have to look at what they want and build a better airline that's relevant to the customer."[9]

Two simple questions help challenge the conventional wisdom that companies need to offer a customer loyalty program and that these programs are worthwhile:

- Are loyal customers *less profitable* for you than disloyal ones?

- Are loyal customers worth the investment required to attract them and maintain them?

Evidence from independent research and from our project work in the United States and Europe indicates that the answer to the first question may indeed be yes and the answer to the second question is often no.

The link between loyalty and profit sounds so nice and so logical that few managers bother to do the math and find out whether loyal customers are profitable customers. They leave this critical assumption unchallenged and rely on their conventional wisdom. The editors of *Harvard Business Review* raised this issue in the July 2002 article "Questioning the Unquestionable." Werner Reinartz of INSEAD and V. Kumar of the University of Connecticut examined data from a U.S. technology service provider, a U.S. direct mail company, a French food retailer, and a German financial services firm. They found no significant link between customer loyalty and customer profitability.

"Specifically, we discovered little or no evidence that customers who purchase steadily from a company over time are necessarily cheaper to serve, less price sensitive, or particularly effective at bringing in new business," they wrote.[10] That does not mean that loyalty means nothing. Rather, it challenges managers to resist blanket statements such as "Loyalty is good" and find out for themselves whether it applies in their case.

The following case shows how a company scrapped plans for loyalty discounts. The quantitative evidence the company gathered showed that introducing a loyalty discount was unnecessary.

Issue: Whether to Introduce a Loyalty Discount to Reward Large Customers

Company: Appleton, Inc.
Product: Packaged software
Source: Simon-Kucher & Partners project

Appleton provides customers with a software package that enables them to reconfigure their workplace. This company had a successful but maturing product line and wanted to know whether it could generate more revenue from existing customers.

Loyal purchasers in this industry insisted on exacting some kind of discount from the list price, so the company could not quickly switch to another pricing model by eliminating all discounts overnight. But the company wondered if it could change the amount of discount. How much discount did the loyal customers deserve? How appropriate would a loyalty discount be?[11]

The company had considered offering customers a better deal on their next purchase, in order to help cement the relationship with them. But it was unsure how large such a discount should be. If the "loyalty" discount were too large, the company would not generate more profit, because increased sales volume might not produce enough revenue. If the company offered no loyalty discount and even tightened existing discounts, it might risk a backlash and likewise fail to capture additional profit.

Appleton's marketing team believed that customers expected a better deal if they had an installed base or had a long track record of consistent purchases. Because the company depended on repeat business, it would put its growth prospects at considerable risk if it denied this advantage to customers who bought regularly. At the same time, the marketing team didn't know whether to believe anecdotal evidence from customers. According to that evidence, the more Appleton software they had installed, the greater the value to them.

To test its loyalty hypotheses, the company needed to learn whether customers who had an installed base of Appleton software had a different willingness to pay than the company's newer customers. In this case, Appleton equated large customers with loyal ones, because nearly all of its key accounts had built up their installed base with regular purchases over a period of years. Using the value measurement techniques described in chapter 5, the company surveyed customers in three countries. The results revealed no relationship between the history of previous purchases and the unit price customers would pay. In the only region where a slight relationship existed, the trend was in fact positive. Customers' willingness to pay for Appleton's products actually *increased* with each subsequent purchase, confirming the anecdotal evidence in the marketplace.

The greater the amount its customers had bought, the greater the gap between the prices they paid and the prices they were willing to pay. Appleton estimated its untapped incremental profit at several million dollars per year, not just in the first year, but over a five-year period. It abandoned plans for a loyalty discount, and gradually reduced the discounts offered on its main product line in order to keep the changes off of customers' radar screens. The company ended its fiscal year with a healthy 12 percent revenue increase. At the same time, it improved its operating margin by 4.5 percentage points, to just under 25 percent. This meant that operating profit rose by 35 percent in absolute terms.

Resist the Urge to Cut Prices Proactively

By arguing against price cuts as a form of competitive reaction when you perceive a competitive threat, we hope to convince you to plan your responses more carefully and consciously by thinking through the consequences first. In some situations, your competitor may force you to make this decision, because it has cut prices itself or entered your market at a much lower price point. We described how to respond to this in the Mosella case in chapter 2.

But in other situations, companies decide to cut prices voluntarily, with no prompting from competitors and—as we show in this section—hardly any prompting from customers either. They decide to cut their prices out of sheer devotion to the idea that lower prices will revive their customers' wavering devotion and ultimately make the company better off. To defend the cuts, they cite changes in the competitive landscape, the convictions of upper management, a willingness to share cost savings and productivity improvements with customers, and the passage in their Economics 101 textbook that said lower prices result in higher volumes. Because price cuts seem to offer the easiest way to lavish special treatment on customers, companies find the temptation hard to resist.

But resist they should. Proactive price cuts don't make you different, nor do they make you better off. They make you poorer, unless you have the evidence, the data, and the math to prove otherwise.

This holds true regardless of how you cut prices. You can cut them through outright price reductions, by offering coupons or cashback incentives, and by heaping services upon your customers in order to clinch a deal or cling to an existing customer relationship. The people making these decisions defend them with platitudes like "The customer is always right" or "We always go the extra mile." Or they rattle off magazine covers that sing the praises of Wal-Mart, Southwest Airlines, and Dell Computer. The argument seems straightforward: if you read that Sam Walton and Michael Dell became billionaires by selling products at bargain-basement prices, why can't you do the same thing in your business?

The reason you can neither quickly nor easily replicate the success of Wal-Mart, Southwest Airlines, and Dell Computer is that they have achieved a cost advantage so large that no company could easily rival them. They also baked this advantage into their business model from Day One. There can only be one cost leader in the industry. To have Southwest's or Wal-Mart's ability to offer low prices, you would need a significant and sustainable cost advantage. We doubt that you have that advantage now, nor will you achieve it in the short term, if ever. If you operate in a mature industry in which competitors offer similar products based on similar technology and inputs, it may even be impossible for any company to achieve more than a slight cost advantage.

And even if you had that ability, why would you use it? Cutting prices almost always amounts to a huge transfer of wealth from corporate stakeholders to customers. You run a company, not a charity. But you show your charitable side when your decision to cut prices reflects entrenched political or philosophical motives, not objective ones. The following case shows how some straightforward math could have prevented a company from making a highly publicized price cut that backfired.

CASE STUDY

Issue: Whether to Cut Prices

Company: Universal Music Group
Product: Compact discs
Source: Analysis of publicly available information

Universal Music Group (UMG), which controlled roughly one-third of the North American market for recorded music, announced in September 2003 that it had cut the suggested retail prices and wholesale prices of compact discs by 25 to 30 percent.[12] It cited consumer research that showed a strong preference at a price point well below its current price levels. It had also concluded that the threat of online piracy not only had persisted, but had fundamentally changed the way certain customers segments buy music.

None of its competitors responded with similar price cuts (a very prescient reaction!), so UMG was free to observe just how strongly a price cut will drive consumer demand. UMG cut the wholesale prices for most of its artists' compact discs to $9.09 from $12.02 to bring people back into the music stores. The goal of this initiative, called JumpStart by the company, seems to have been to provide customers with a clear incentive to return to the traditional way of buying music.

One commentary said that UMG's decision "seems less a savvy attempt to fight back and more a last-ditch effort to avoid losing any further ground."[13] Following the price cut, UMG would have needed to ship 33 percent more CD units just to maintain the same amount of revenue. Achieving the same amount of *profit* presented an even greater challenge. Depending on what assumptions you make about variable costs, UMG would have needed to sell between 45 and 55 percent more CDs to break even. Where was all the customer demand before the price cuts? Can a lower price point really make that many artists that hot? You might argue that UMG would have seen lower profits anyway, if it had done nothing. But even when you take the "do nothing" scenario with a volume decline into account, UMG would have been much better off without the price cuts.

UMG also fell victim to the law of unexpected consequences. In our experience, managers often neglect to ask the question of whether their price changes will contaminate their future dealings with distributors and customers. Nor do they ask how someone could use their price cut as a weapon against them. The *New York Times* reported that the cut in suggested retail prices, combined with a less steep cut in wholesale prices, could cause retailers to shift shelf space away from CDs to other products.[14] At the time of the price cuts, Wal-Mart had already planned to reduce the space it devoted to music by 15 percent because of slow sales and low profits, the story said. UMG also shifted its marketing dollars away from in-store promotions and toward advertising directly to consumers. This move could accelerate the demise of smaller and specialty chains. These developments are rather ironic when you consider that Doug Morris, Universal Music's CEO and chairman, said upon announcing the price cuts that "we are making a bold move to bring people back to music stores."[15]

Finally, exactly whom was Morris trying to lure back into the music stores? You might think it is the old Napster-Kazaa crowd, which came of age by downloading music for free and could be defined as the fifteen to twenty-four age group.

But according to the Recording Industry Association of America (RIAA), that demographic group accounted for only 25 percent of all music purchases, down from 32 percent in the early 1990s. The age group thirty-five and older accounts for nearly half of all purchases (45.2 percent), up from roughly a third (33.7 percent) a decade earlier.[16]

If nearly half of all music buyers in the United States haven't seen a high school classroom in almost twenty years, these are probably not people who have abandoned retail stores. Instead, these are the same people who pay hundreds of dollars for Bruce Springsteen or Rolling Stones tickets, or the bundle of Rolling Stones and Fleetwood Mac tickets we used as an example in chapter 6. They have a proven willingness to pay for music.

A few months after the price cuts, UMG executives "conceded that the price-cut program has not yet been successful."[17] Instead of boosting unit sales and bringing customers back into music stores, the price cut appeared to have no effect at all. Universal's market share in both new releases and overall had actually fallen slightly.

After waiting almost a year for its original plan to work, UMG "partially retreated from many of the price cuts."[18] The company originally expected JumpStart to boost volume by 21 percent. It achieved that only for "carryover" CDs, or those on the market for more than eight weeks but less than two years. That segment grew by 27 percent in volume. New releases, though, grew by only 5.8 percent, and sales of older CDs by just 3 percent. UMG officials said that the plan did not work because retailers did not cooperate as expected by passing on the price cuts.

What other alternatives did UMG's Morris have? He had several viable ones, as described in chapters 6 and 7. He could have raised prices indirectly. Sony Music, one of Universal's main rivals, has kept CD prices steady, but has reduced the number of tracks on some discs. On a per-song basis, this amounts to a price increase. Howard Stringer, at that time the chairman and CEO of Sony Corporation of America, said that consumers actually prefer fewer tracks on each CD, and added that putting fewer tracks on a CD could speed up the next release by the artist.[19] Although this reflects a price increase— customers get less for their money and spend more often—it does not hurt them as long as the artist remains popular. This move reflects a return to the way record companies released albums decades ago. In the 1960s, rock-and-roll bands released smaller albums more frequently than they do today.

UMG could have raised prices directly. Had Morris mimicked AOL's approach and raised prices directly, we would argue strongly that he not only would have generated continued strong revenues from older music buyers, but also would have made his business more attractive to retailers.

Finally, UMG could have used a preference-based segmentation instead of taking a shotgun approach with the price reduction. As the results suggested, price cuts did make sense to some degree for carryover CDs. A strategy of "Price cuts for everybody!" does permanent damage to your price integrity as well as your profitability. Porsche's CEO Wendelin Wiedeking defined price integrity and summarized its importance in *Automotive News.* "Once you have sold a car with high rebates to a customer, he comes back and wants the same deal again. You'll never be able to make this customer happy, because he will say your pricing is wrong."[20] But sometimes even Porsche carefully uses incentives to reduce inventories. The trick is this: most people don't know about them. For several months, Porsche offered $2,000 to $3,500 cash rebates on 911 and Boxster models. But it offered these incentives only to current Porsche owners and never advertised them.[21]

When momentum in favor of a price cut or loyalty incentive grows within your company, take a "guilty until proven innocent" approach. The burden of proof must rest with the advocates of the price cut or loyalty incentive. Their proof must have hard profit numbers to support it, not just political weight or philosophical conviction.

Summary

You should not overindulge your customer. Instead, make sure that you extract fair value for what you deliver. Aggressive and acquiescent actions hinder your own efforts to pursue higher profits. The actions shown in figure 8-1—customer giveaways, value attacks, and aggressive price cuts—represent a huge transfer of wealth from you to your customers.

Value attacks occur when you provide customers with increasingly better quality, but fail to charge for it adequately. Loyalty programs make sense only when competitors cannot easily duplicate them, which means they cannot provide the same benefits to the same degree. Even then, you need to do the math to make sure the investment in loyalty programs earns a sufficient return.

Price cuts make sense only when they earn you higher profits. Most don't. When the Toronto Blue Jays lowered some prices in the case in chapter 7, they had hard analyses to show that the lower prices in certain sections would earn them more money. It is unlikely that Universal Music Group had similar analyses in the case in this chapter.

Take a guilty-until-proven-innocent approach when someone suggests that you offer a customer giveaway, make a value attack, or cut prices. The risks to your profit are too great.

Keeping your team on the path to higher profits requires more than rhetoric. It demands the alignment of goals across the organization, with incentives to cement that alignment. Chapter 9 explores this area.

CHAPTER 9

Align Your Incentives
to Focus on Profit

*You don't understand my problem. You're trying to show me
how to grow profits, how to put more sacks of money on the table.
My problem is that management is not thinking in terms of
sacks of money; they're putting 1 million units of product
on that table and saying, "Here, sell these!"*
—Global sales manager of a multinational corporation[1]

To RETRIEVE the higher profits they deserve, companies need to make the transition from volume-based sales incentive systems to profit-based ones. This applies to your own sales representatives and to your channel partners, who act as your agents at the end customer.

Help Your Salespeople Convince Customers to Pay Higher Prices, Not Fight Their Superiors to Grant Lower Prices

Senior management plays a crucial role in making these incentives work. Part of your corporate communication includes consistent messages about your commitment to the profit targets. If you decide to reward salespeople according to the profit they generate for the company instead of the volume they sell, you cannot continue to project the idea that market share is still your top priority and set corporate goals accordingly. Otherwise, you put your salespeople in a no-win situation. They receive mixed signals on what matters, and will transmit those mixed signals to the market through their actions.

When companies have a limited number of products, all of which contribute significantly to revenue and profit, the goal conflicts become magnified when it is unclear who has pricing authority. One of the world's leading logistics companies, which we'll call Depardo, tried to test its pricing power, but without taking goal conflicts into account. It enacted an across-the-board price increase of 2 percent. You can imagine its surprise when management noticed after a few months that average transaction prices had actually *fallen* by 1.5 percent.[2]

CASE STUDY

Issue: Encourage Salespeople to Discount Less

Company: Depardo
Product: Express delivery
Source: Simon-Kucher & Partners project

Depardo's sales force responded to the price increase by testing its own pricing power. Guess who won. Salespeople resisted the price increase because it made their life tougher in a market where several other well-known multinational companies competed aggressively for business. But they did not simply say no and tear up their price sheets in protest. They took their case to customers by showing them the new price list and then encouraging them to shift to more favorable discount brackets. This was possible because customers negotiated volume rebates in advance based on planned volume. Depardo rarely checked actual volumes after the fact to see if they matched up.

Let's say that a customer bought eighty thousand units in the previous year, which entitled them to a discount of 3 percent. In the sales discussion for the coming year's business, a Depardo salesperson might have approached a purchaser with the following argument: "You plan to grow next year, right? If you can stretch things so that you buy one hundred thousand units, we can lock in the discount at the higher bracket, which is 6 percent." The purchaser said that one hundred thousand units matched up well with the company's growth target, and one handshake later the deal was done.

If the customer never reached the target of one hundred thousand units, Depardo usually did not rescind the discount. As a result of many situations like this one, average unit prices fell by 1.5 percent instead of rising by 2 percent as planned. This swing of 3.5 percent had a dramatic effect on profits.

The structure of Depardo's discount system certainly played a role. Depardo paid sales commissions according to revenue and revenue growth. A salesperson's prestige grew in proportion to the number of deals closed or the amount of new business brought in. Salespeople had no incentive to behave otherwise, regardless of what discount system Depardo had on paper. This particular system just made it easier for them. To say that these people did not really care much about price or profit is not cynicism. It is reality. It was built into the system.

Who suffers when that happens? The highly qualified and competent people running Depardo's operating units never felt the pain, because no one ever made it clear to them that they could realize considerably higher profits if they fixed the problem. Because of the resulting price contamination, these managers had unwittingly caused their profit potential in the market to evaporate. Once a company lowers its prices in the logistics market, it rarely has an opportunity to raise them again. The money that the higher prices would have generated is gone. As with the airlines, the repercussions may last for years to come.

Given the degree of resistance in the organization, Depardo has made slow but steady progress in incorporating profit-based incentives for salespeople. Because of the extreme complexity and interdependencies in their business, they have not yet succeeded in instituting a cleaner profit-based system like the ones we describe in the next section. But the new incentive system has at least stemmed the decline in prices and made salespeople and managers more sensitive to the effect that lower prices have on corporate profits and on their own pay.

Get the Monetary Incentives Right: Hard Cash Still Matters

Your organizational structure doesn't matter if you don't have the proper incentives in place to make the right things happen. The problem often lies in the fact that managers focus more on how much people get paid than on how people get rewarded in other ways such as through honors, status, and career advancement opportunities. If you are paid according to profit, but your CEO is really after market share—regardless of what your vision and mission statement may say—you will have to make a personal and professional trade-off.

How do you change a compensation system to defuse these conflicts? You could initiate a collaborative effort between sales and management to resolve an entrenched goal conflict, as Kinston did in the case described in chapter 5.

In that chapter, we described how Kinston used a mix of expert judgment, analysis of internal data, and customer research to develop a guidance tool for salespeople. This tool did not show the price elasticities the salesperson needed as numbers, but rather as icons that denoted whether the customer segment was very sensitive, neutral, or rather insensitive to prices for the particular product group.

To ensure compliance, Kinston integrated the new tool with its incentives for salespeople. The old incentive system rewarded salespeople according to the amount of revenue they generated. Driven to achieve the highest commissions they could, the sales team decided to strike deals even when they knew they would have to make substantial concessions on price. The system would have given salespeople no clear reason—at least no monetary one—to change their behavior and defend higher price levels under the new system. Kinston wanted to break this habit quickly, cleanly, and permanently.

The company encouraged use of this new tool by creating an incentive for price defense. The structure was quite simple. The higher the discount a salesperson granted, the lower his or her commission would be. Using gross profits as a basis for the commission would have had a similar effect. Many companies, however, feel uncomfortable in sharing product-specific gross profit levels with hundreds or thousands of salespeople. Taking the discount level is a reasonable proxy. The salespeople could also see the monetary amount of their commission directly on their laptop screen, so they could see in real time how much money they would lose if they relented on price. The coded information on price elasticity, meanwhile, would give them the confidence to hold their ground if they were dealing with a customer with relatively low price sensitivity.

The effect of the new system was strong and swift. The average discount the sales team granted dropped to 14 percent from 16 percent in a matter of weeks, with hardly any customer defections or loss in volume. These extra two percentage points resulted in incremental profit estimated at about $100 million. Considering that the entire project, including IT implementation and sales force training, cost around $1 million, Kinston could measure the payback period of the project in a handful of days.

The strategic dimension of the compensation structure also matters. Inevitably, your new competition map (as described in chapter 2) will tell some of your salespeople that they need to back off of certain customers or customer segments. Since they are not responsible for this shift in priorities, they should not pay for it. Do not forget to compensate them for business they have to shed.

After a company we'll call Randolph Partners decided to end its longstanding internal conflict between volume and profit goals, it took an approach similar to Kinston's, but implemented a somewhat more complicated incentive scheme.

CASE STUDY

Issue: Encourage Salespeople to Discount Less

Company: Randolph Partners
Product: Industrial services
Source: Simon-Kucher & Partners project

Money played a significant role in the compensation for salespeople at Randolph. Traditionally, the company built its incentive system for salespeople around the revenue and revenue growth that an individual or a team achieved in a given year. In contrast, the variable compensation for key account managers and global account managers derived from the *margins* the company achieved, not the revenue.[3]

The goal conflict seemed obvious enough. You might wonder why Randolph would have kept a system destined to create a behavioral conflict between salespeople and their managers. In fact, Randolph had a very logical reason for this system: it wanted to prevent sensitive internal information from turning up on competitors' desks. Turnover among salespeople was high, with many of them lured away by Randolph's expansion-minded competitors. Making margin information available to the rank-and-file salespeople would essentially shed light on the company's cost structure. Randolph wanted to reserve this information for upper management.

But basing sales incentives entirely on revenue also brings disadvantages. Offering higher discounts to win business or lock in higher volumes became standard practice, with progressively gloomier consequences for Randolph as a whole. Margins fell in lockstep with prices to the extent that a significant part of the company's business became unprofitable.

How bad was the problem? Discount levels exceeded the levels prescribed in the discount guidelines in almost two-thirds of all deals. Yet Randolph could not blame the salespeople for this. As they should, they acted in their own interests within the incentive structure Randolph offered them. But this natural tendency to act in line with incentives explains only part of what happened. Some customers had begun to buy less over time, yet Randolph did not alter its terms. The company focused entirely on revenue without systematically looking at revenue quality.

Randolph faced a dilemma. How could it change the incentive system for employees without revealing confidential information? It felt that if that information really did leave the company, the solution could be worse than the problem itself. To resolve the dilemma, Randolph based the incentive payment on several components. One of those components would focus on the discount level itself, rather than on the level of profit that resulted from it. Each salesperson and sales team would agree on certain targets at the beginning of the year. They could then earn incentives—expressed as a percentage of their fixed salary—based on what they sold and what prices they achieved.

Unlike in the previous system, the individual salespeople or managers received the amount only if they reached the agreed target, measured against the effective discount rate based on all their transactions. This hurdle was all or nothing. If the salespeople were too generous and fell short of their goal, they received no premium at all. But if they exceeded their goal by pushing through lower-than-expected discounts, their payouts grew proportionately.

The system would still offer the sales teams the opportunity to earn substantially more than their fixed salary. In fact, the total payout in the old and new systems would be roughly equal in absolute dollar terms. The new system, though, had one important difference: it increased resistance along the previous path of least resistance. Salespeople who insisted on using lower prices to drive volume would literally take money out of their own pockets. If they changed their behavior to fit the company's overall goals, they would receive ample reward.

This system allowed Randolph's management to differentiate goals by product. Products in mature markets received tougher targets, while new products received softer targets as Randolph tried to establish them.

Randolph's sales teams demonstrated a willingness to change. They accepted the new system. To ease the transition, Randolph management set relatively conservative goals in the first few quarters. Because the discount component had an all-or-nothing character, the whole system would have collapsed if very challenging or unrealistic goals had discouraged participation and kept the salespeople from having that first taste of success.

Randolph had resolved the dilemma by aligning incentive systems with corporate goals in a way that salespeople could appreciate. The actual features of the new system, however, are only half of the story. The system could not have succeeded without two other factors: speed and investment. Randolph developed and implemented the solution quickly, without having to bankroll new investments in information technology. Once again, the mental investment trumped the monetary one.

The project to refine the system took eight months. Randolph assembled a team from pricing, sales, sales promotion, and IT that created the new concept. The IT representatives played a critical role, because the cost of purchasing and implementing a new software solution could have delayed or even undermined the process. To make the system work, all salespeople needed immediate access to how close they were to meeting their personal target for the quarter. They required a means to compare their target with a weighted average of the discounts on all their transactions, but the existing IT system did not allow that. Fortunately, the IT team saw a link to a parallel project meant to develop a tool to monitor customer volume and revenue. By integrating one extra field for the "effective discount," the IT team could piggyback on the other project.

Reward Channel Partners for Performance, Not Just for Volume

A power tool manufacturer we'll call Acorn Holdings offered its distributors a standard discount of 37 percent off list prices.[4] The distributors could then charge end customers whatever they wanted and earn their profit accordingly. According to the volume they sold, they would also be eligible for an annual rebate.

Sometimes, however, the distributors felt that the 37 percent discount did not leave them enough breathing room to close a deal. To deal with these "exceptions" in a uniform way, Acorn established an escalation process. If distributors needed a higher discount level—say, in order to close a deal with an important or more price-sensitive customer boasting a lower bid from a competitor—they could receive up to 43 percent without going through a formal approval process. But in return, Acorn would reduce the amount of annual rebate the distributor could earn. The higher the discount became, the lower the rebate would be. Fearing that distributors could abuse this process, Acorn's managers tried to discourage them from seeking an exception by requiring them to submit documentation of the final deal. They also selectively audited distributors.

If distributors needed a discount beyond 43 percent, they had to provide proof that they needed the lower price in order to get formal written approval from Acorn's management. Such deals would not count toward the year-end rebate at all.

CASE STUDY

Issue: Cut Down on Price "Exceptions" for Channel Partners

Company: Acorn Holdings
Product: Power tools
Source: Simon-Kucher & Partners project

When we examined the discount levels on every deal, we saw two very prominent clusters at 37 percent and 43 percent. Together, they accounted for more than half of all transactions and nearly all of the exceptions. You may have expected that result at 37 percent. The intriguing finding, though, is the nearly complete lack of transactions between 38 and 42 percent. Even though the distributors would have earned a higher year-end rebate if they had bought the product at, say, 41 percent off instead of 43 percent off, they ignored that extra monetary incentive entirely and simply focused on obtaining the lowest available price that did not require much extra effort. Apparently, the incentive of a higher rebate—combined with the disincentive of documentation and audits—was not strong enough to entice them to defend higher price levels.

The more intriguing finding emerged, though, when the company modified its discount structure the following year in conjunction with an increase in list prices. It eliminated the barrier at 37 percent and instead introduced a two-step approval process. All discounts below 43 percent would require Acorn's approval on the basis of a more rigorous defense of why the lower price was necessary. All requests for discounts beyond 47 percent would require the approval of Acorn's divisional vice president. The resulting sales would earn the distributor no rebate whatsoever.

When we plotted the discount levels for all deals for that subsequent year, we saw the same phenomenon. Distributors simply looked at how Acorn had structured the new "game" and played accordingly. Distributors essentially ignored the monetary incentives designed to encourage them to sell at higher prices. Why did they ignore the incentive and abuse the system? They simply did not need the rebate incentive, because they made the bulk of their money with maintenance, ancillary supplies, and follow-on services. Their interest in gaining another service customer—and the associated stream of consistent revenue—far outweighed the few extra dollars they would earn from Acorn by fighting for a higher price on the initial sale.

Acorn decided to scrap its system instead of making it harder to abuse. It decided to use more positive incentives to steer people in the right direction instead of using more control mechanisms to keep people in line when the underlying system failed. The rationale showed considerable common sense. Its management felt that the only way to make the old system better—in terms of profit for Acorn—would mean making it worse in every other way: more paperwork, more time, more staff to handle the exceptions, and more training. For the new system, it used the kind of functional incentive system quite common in the automotive industry. We refer to this as "managing the dealer instead of managing the deal."

Under this model, lower prices for dealers or distributors would be contingent upon fulfilling minimum standards in certain areas, such as store appearance, salesperson certification, and an independent measure of customer satisfaction. The company also limited price exceptions solely to high-volume purchases from existing customers. Acorn also decided to shift some of the money it formerly "invested" in discounts into tactical promotions to clear inventory or to help distributors correct temporary imbalances. After some resistance, the distributors accepted the new system. Acorn saw far fewer exceptions because the distributors' sales skills with the end customers took priority, not their ability to play the exceptions game with their own supplier.

Lead by Example If You Want a Culture of Profit

In mature markets, higher market share and higher profit are incompatible goals. If you try to boost profit, you need a way to keep people from becoming nervous the moment your volume drops.

The chief sales officer of the private banking division of one of the world's largest banks showed that nervousness when the CEO put him under strong pressure to increase profits. He feared a backlash if he lost customers. We asked him what the consequences would be if his account managers raised prices high enough to boost annual total profit by 20 percent, but at the same time lost 5 percent of their customers.[5]

"This is really difficult," he responded. "Even with the much higher profits, I would have a hard time explaining to upper management why 5 percent of our wealthiest customers took their business elsewhere."

If the highest level of management cannot decide what it wants, how can it expect salespeople to act consistently and in line with corporate goals? Given this unavoidable tension, it is impossible to convince your organization to capture your opportunities for higher profits when you continue to reward your salespeople—directly or indirectly—for achieving volume targets. If you do this, you overemphasize one variable in the profit equation (volume) rather than profit itself. We do acknowledge that the company with the largest market share is often likely to be the most profitable one in its industry, at least for a certain period. But let us not confuse cause and effect: does this high market share itself drive sustained higher profits, or is the company merely basking in the warm afterglow of the days when it had the far superior product that catapulted it to leadership in the first place? It makes a big difference whether a company grows and then maintains its market share through a superior product, service, or brand, or through aggressive price cuts.

As markets mature, market share levels become stickier. Innovation is the best way to change them or extend them significantly, but true innovations are rare. It follows that in fiercely competitive markets full of established products, a company should focus on differentiation and pursue the higher profits it deserves. To do anything else will unnecessarily lower the profit potential in the market.

We want to encourage you not only to embrace the idea of a greater profit orientation but also to "live" that idea in your company. But how do you achieve this orientation in the short term and make it stick for the long term?

A manager accepting that challenge has little chance to succeed if he or she does not identify goal conflicts within the organization and resolve them. Almost every company has two sets of goals to obey: the ones codified in the company's vision statements and handbooks, and de facto goals, the unwritten ones projected by top management through its actions and its moods. The problems start when these goals do not match.

Goal conflicts work insidiously to impair a company's ability to function. They interfere with cross-selling efforts, because they prevent companies from properly sharing the credit and the money when a sale is made. They reduce effectiveness and transparency, because people are reluctant to speak up or exchange information. They stifle initiative, because the rewards for taking chances are not clear. These conflicts can even distort market signals, because they encourage sales teams to push product out the door at absurdly favorable terms just for the sake of making a sale. Taken together, goal conflicts almost always succeed in doing one thing: reducing a company's ability to earn the higher profits it deserves.

Understanding and resolving goal conflicts will involve changing the resistance along the various paths your employees take to earn not only money, prestige, and status, but also personal satisfaction and a whole list of other motivators—even profit.

"Big bang" actions to put new incentive systems in place may make sense on paper, but they can create a culture of uncertainty. Salespeople will assume that if management had the nerve to launch one sudden overhaul, nothing will prevent it from doing so again. The actions of the electronics goods retailer Circuit City show how management can breed that uncertainty by changing the rules overnight.

In February 2003, some thirty-nine hundred highly paid commissioned salespeople at Circuit City lost their jobs.[6] The move came as such a surprise that an account of it in the *Wall Street Journal* included the subheadline "I was so good, I got fired." The article soberly described the disconnect between the salespeople's expectations and management's actions: "Some expected to be told that their commissions would be cut. Instead, they were given their walking papers. They simply made too much money at a time when the company was desperate to economize."[7]

One salesman had sold more than $1 million in computers and consumer electronics in one year. That earned him $54,000 in salary and bonuses and a place in the President's Club for top salesmen. Circuit City dismissed him. The company expected that laying off the high-paid salespeople, plus two hundred repair personnel, would save it $130 million annually.

Laying off people always lowers morale considerably. But a decision such as Circuit City's risks destroying employee confidence. They punished the people who responded best to their incentives. This makes people wary of following the next system or the next set of instructions. It makes one wonder what will happen with Circuit City's next incentive system.

Summary

A common corporate shortcut is to reward salespeople primarily on how much they sell (volume) or how much revenue they bring in. This shortcut often encourages behavior that can destroy your profits or undermine your efforts to increase them. It trains salespeople to ask their superiors for lower prices instead of negotiating with customers for higher ones.

Overcoming these shortcut incentives is difficult because of conflicting goals. They reflect the critical conflict we introduced in chapter 1: whether to pursue higher market share or higher profit. Until you focus on profit and align everyone's incentives around that goal, you are setting yourself up for failure.

When you want to provide incentives to your employees, cash rewards are important but not the whole story. Incentives should also recognize people's need for higher status and prestige. How you reward channel partners should be similar to how you reward salespeople. You should reward them for actions that help you earn more money, rather than giving them cash discounts or rebates based entirely on volume.

Establishing a culture of profitability in a company begins at the very top. You need to project that culture of profit inside your company and outside it as well. Harnessing your market communications—both words and actions—will ensure that the message resonates. Chapter 10 shows how to get your market communications under control.

CHAPTER 10

Get Your Market
Communication Under Control

Make no mistake.
We are not going to back off one inch on this vehicle.

—Steve Lyons, head of the Ford division of
Ford Motor Company, commenting on the
launch of the new F-150 pickup truck[1]

A T THE BEGINNING of this book, we described some of the
daily challenges managers in mature markets face. We also
noted that through their words and actions, managers can exert considerable influence on their markets, whether intended or not. This
fact alone means that managers should take careful and conscious
control of what they say in public. They need to understand how
public statements can help them secure their profit opportunities,
and how miscommunication or lack of communication can jeopardize them. This is especially true for smaller companies, which do
not have the same access to public relations experts and legal counsel
as larger companies do.

The bulk of the material in the previous chapters focused on
things you can *do* to earn the higher profits you deserve. This final
chapter emphasizes things you can *say*.

Make Sure You Say What You Mean
When You Make Public Statements

As we discussed in chapter 2, your competitors are not automatically your mortal enemies. But that does not imply that they are your friends. Initiating a dialogue might certainly solve many of your problems, but it would also land you in prison. Antitrust laws prohibit such discussions, especially when they involve price.

But you can still make your concerns and frustrations public, as the head of the mobile-phone division of Siemens, one of the top-five handset makers in the world, did. After planning responses to recent price cuts announced by Nokia, he commented that "naturally one of these [responses] is to bring down prices . . . but I won't allow myself to be drawn into an irrational price war."[2] Hewlett-Packard took a similar but less blunt approach when it announced that it would cede market share to its main competitor, Dell, in order to preserve profits.[3]

Nokia and Hewlett-Packard have sent signals to their markets. Michael Porter defines a market signal as "any action by a competitor that provides a direct or indirect indication of its intentions, motives, goals, or internal situation."[4] Companies of all shapes and sizes send signals for all sorts of products. Many of them are straightforward and easy to understand.

Porter's definition, however, underscores the difficulty companies have in sending signals. Every action you take in the marketplace, and every statement your executives or managers make publicly, sends a signal, whether you like it or not. Your customers, investors, and competitors may ignore the ones you wanted to send, and misinterpret harmless statements and actions on your part. The following anecdote shows how such confusion can come about:

> Northwest, like its rival old-line airlines, has a pricing department built on incredibly sophisticated computer models and

an army of financial analysts, all of which produces, as might be expected, incredibly complicated pricing. Airlines change prices as many as seven times a day on thousands of fares, and analysts try to decipher competitors' strategies, shifts and signals, fare-by-fare, day-by-day, minute-by-minute.

When an ex-Southwest worker showed up, his new employer quickly asked a question that had long troubled Northwest. Southwest only responded to pricing changes on Tuesdays. What did that mean? What signal was Southwest trying to send to the rest of the industry?

"We only met on Tuesdays," the new employee shrugged.[5]

Signaling in the form of broad-based market communication is nonetheless a fast, effective, and legal way to inform your market of your plans and intentions, or let the market know that that you felt someone has made a dangerously bad decision. As a pleasant side effect, it may serve to preempt other companies from taking actions that may destroy your profits. You should make your statements in such a way that they can reach customers, competitors, investors, analysts, and in some cases even regulators.

Send Positive Signals to Keep a "Cold" Marketing War from Heating Up

Companies that send positive signals are trying to define what they want in the market, what they feel they deserve, what kind of resistance they will tolerate, and what kind of resistance will prompt retaliation. The largest battleground for vehicles in North America—and where the manufacturers earn most of their money—is the pickup truck. Competitors in that market regularly send positive signals. The signaling process for the latest version of Ford's perennially strong F-150 pickup began in earnest even before Ford launched it.

Issue: How to Communicate Your Marketing Goals

Companies: Ford and General Motors
Product: Pickup trucks
Source: Analysis of publicly available information

Steve Lyons's quote at the start of this section encapsulates Ford's stance on competition in this segment. But throughout the introductory period, Lyons engaged his counterpart Gary White, a vehicle line executive at General Motors, in a fascinating give-and-take. They never spoke directly, but their comments became public in articles by *Wall Street Journal* reporter Norihiko Shirouzu. The articles revealed two managers who seemed driven primarily by market share and volume targets.

Shirouzu quoted Lyons as saying that Ford wanted to increase the volume of its F-Series to 1 million units, versus 813,700 units the year before. Reaching the seven-figure plateau in unit sales would "be kind of fun. Nobody sold a million of anything for quite a while."[6] Does this sound like an aggressive claim to conquer the North American pickup truck market? No, it seemed more like the lukewarm public acknowledgement of some internal Ford goals to increase market share, and not something that competitors should view as a real threat.

Later that year, Lyons told the reporter that he anticipated General Motors would offer big discounts on the Chevrolet Silverado and GMC Sierra in order to torpedo Ford's relaunch of its F-150.

In a separate interview, White said that GM would fight to "keep its leadership in the big pickup segment."[7] To fend off the perceived threat from GM, Ford would continue to produce the old F-150 and use it as a weapon in a price war.

"If you want to discount yours, we'll discount ours," Lyons was quoted as saying, adding that this situation was "high stakes poker."[8] This signal was in line with the first one: Lyons made it implicitly clear that he was not really after expanding the F-150's share, but he was absolutely adamant about not willing to accept a loss.

Yes, this is high stakes poker, but with investors' money. Given the amount of profits, jobs, and ego at stake, both Lyons and White knew they needed to tread carefully. In their public statements, both basically sketched out a satisfactory solution: If you don't attack me, I will not attack you.

Comments Lyons made later in *CFO Magazine* confirm that he may talk like an aggressor, but he doesn't necessarily act like one. When General Motors supplemented its generous incentive program by adding a loyalty discount of $1,000 on top of its 0 percent financing and large cash incentives, Ford did not respond. Ford decided to "let them get a short-term boost, and resist giving away the sun, the moon, and the stars," Lyons was quoted as saying. "Next month they'll struggle and we'll have the right product at the right price."[9]

Send Neutral Signals to Tell the Market
to Prepare for Your Pending Actions

Companies send neutral signals to tell the market well in advance what they have planned, in order to keep the market from overreacting or misjudging the situation when their preannounced move actually takes place. This section describes signals sent by IKEA, Ryanair, and America Online.

IKEA, the world's largest and most profitable furniture retailer, strives to maintain the market's lowest prices, but without going to extremes. IKEA has publicly declared that the company cuts its prices as soon as it sees that a rival is cheaper.[10] But in doing so, IKEA preserves the relationship between its own prices and those of its local competitors. IKEA's statement constitutes a signal, a clear message that it will never allow competitors to undercut IKEA's prices.

The threat is credible. IKEA's production capabilities are so vast and its costs so low that it could conceivably undercut all rivals by much more than it actually does. But it chooses to follow a strategy that makes itself more profitable, even if that may mean competitors can earn money as well.

Signaling is nothing new for the airline industry, though some companies send and decode signals better than others. Michael O'Leary, chairman of Ryanair (Europe's equivalent to Southwest Airlines), plans to "destroy European air transportation as we know it" by becoming larger than the established national carriers like British Airways, Air France, and Lufthansa.[11] Would you like to know O'Leary's strategy? He revealed it publicly when he said that Ryanair plans to reduce ticket prices by 5 percent per year over the next five years. That would bring the average price of a Ryanair ticket down from forty-nine euros to just under thirty-eight euros.[12] Of course, O'Leary can revise this guidance at any time. He has no crystal ball. But as chairman of a publicly traded company, he cannot toss out any numbers he likes for public consumption. O'Leary effectively drew a line in the clouds and told his future opponents the prices they would need to beat to challenge him. In a time when all airlines are writing business plans for low-cost carrier alternatives, this line functions as a powerful barrier to entry.

In chapter 7 we analyzed AOL's decision to raise the monthly subscription fee for its traditional dial-up service. If you evaluated the company's service solely on the individual features—such as connection quality, ease of use, and technical options—that it includes, you probably would not rank AOL at the top. Yet in its entirety, the AOL service provided a simple, easy-to-understand way to go online. The mainstream customer found it attractive.

Issue: How to "Test the Waters" Ahead of a Potential Price Increase

Company: America Online
Product: Dial-up Internet service
Source: Analysis of publicly available information

Historically, Internet service providers (ISPs) in the United States set their prices against the benchmark of AOL. After AOL raised the price for basic dial-up service to $23.90 per month, EarthLink opted to match, while Microsoft held prices steady on its MSN service. It became apparent what each competitor sought. EarthLink needed money and MSN wanted market share. NetZero, a low-cost competitor, continued to base its entire positioning on AOL by claiming its service cost half as much as AOL's. AOL had given structure and order to a rapidly growing market.

Had you invested the time to follow America Online's activities after the consummation of the AOL Time Warner merger, you would have known that the price increase would come relatively soon. You only needed to track the public statements AOL officials made and observe how they evolved.[13] Before the actual move, only its precise magnitude remained open.

Unless you believe that all of the statements in figure 10-1 are pure coincidence, you would conclude that AOL conducted a planned signaling campaign. Of course, the signal cynics may question whether all of these statements really made any difference to competitors. They argue that Microsoft and EarthLink would have

FIGURE 10-1

AOL's signaling plan ahead of its price increase

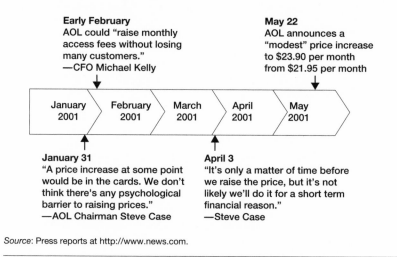

Source: Press reports at http://www.news.com.

made exactly the same decisions regardless of what AOL said in the months preceding the price increase. These comments miss the point.

Put yourself in AOL's position. You see that your costs have risen because of an upsurge in usage by your customers. You see broadband penetration beginning to rise, but you have no response to this threat to your core dial-up service. (In fact, AOL did not announce a broadband strategy until eighteen months after the price increase.) If you make the decision to manage the impending decline of your service by raising prices and shoring up your profits, you need to make some assumptions about how your customers, the investment community, and your competitors might respond. Even if you assume with some certainty that MSN will use your move as an opportunity to gain some market share (but not cut the price on its own), while EarthLink will go for the extra cash, you still face the risk that it won't happen. You face the risk of your competitors behaving irrationally because of time pressure. How can you mitigate that risk? You send signals early on. You give the market ample time to think through its responses or provide an indication of how it might respond, before the action even takes place. You try to build your own confidence that no one will do something rash when the time comes for them to respond.

It is absurd to think that AOL told its competitors what to do, or that anyone at MSN headquarters in Redmond, Washington, needed AOL's assistance in crafting a response. If you have ever seen an EarthLink commercial from that era or received an advertisement from MSN asking you to switch to its service, you will realize that there is no love lost among these rivals. In our view, AOL meant its signals as insurance for the stability of its market. Just as much as it wanted to tell the market about the price increase, it also wanted to tell the market that it wanted stability and market discipline, not turmoil. Why risk sudden shifts in market share to one player or the other when AOL, MSN, and EarthLink all know that such shifts would not be sustainable, since the other player would be forced to retaliate immediately? AOL wanted to make a contribution to stability in its market.

Send Offensive Signals as a Warning
Shot to Force a Retreat

When we discuss signaling with our clients, we often encounter at least one cynic who dismisses the whole notion of signaling as academic blah-blah.

Signaling as part of a marketing strategy just sounds so lame to them. To the cynics, signaling is like hearing that an Arnold Schwarzenegger movie character suddenly set down his sword and shield and instead asked a monk to issue a press release saying,

"Conan the Barbarian now thinks fighting is a waste of time and is happy with his current position in the world." How dramatic is that?

It's not dramatic, the cynics say. A "real" competitor would never play winkie-winkie in the marketplace by issuing a press release or giving interviews to trade magazines in the hope that someone gets the hint. This was business, after all, and not a third-grade classroom.

"No, the only signal anyone understands is pain," they conclude. "Inflict as much of it as possible, until your competitor goes away."

The "us versus them" split in this culture of aggression could hardly be more clear. Aggressors inflict pain, regardless of how badly their own profits might suffer as a result. For them, the medium is the message, and their medium of choice is war. In contrast, the superior performers try to "inflict peace" on their markets. They understand that you can achieve most of your business goals without a rush of adrenaline.

Sometimes even the most peaceful and reserved managers need to inflict pain. Offensive signals allow you to inflict pain in measured doses: if competitors implement something you don't like, sometimes the most effective signal is to strike back. But you must avoid making this a direct confrontation. Instead, focus your counterattack on an area where the competitor will take notice but probably not escalate.

Continental Airlines once responded in this manner to Northwest. In the early 1990s, Northwest Airlines cut its prices on several routes on the U.S. West Coast. The company, however, had not counted on a reaction from Continental Airlines, which had begun to make the U.S. West Coast one of its core markets.

Instead of fighting back on its home field, where it wanted to sustain an advantage, Continental slashed prices to and from Minneapolis, where Northwest had one of its major hubs. Northwest seemed to understand the message and quickly restored prices on the West Coast to their previous levels.[14]

Nearly ten years later, several major airlines abandoned their individual efforts to raise prices $10 each way on most routes because Northwest Airlines decided not to match it on all routes.[15] What were they thinking? How do you deal with a company like Northwest Airlines in your market?

If all that aggressors understand is pain, teaching them a lesson with a surgical strike becomes your last resort. The key is to avoid fighting back where your competitor has attacked you by attacking them directly—and to the same degree—in a market they themselves value.

Issue: How to Respond When a Competitor Enters Your Market

Companies: Continental Materials and Morgan
Product: Specialty insulation
Source: Simon-Kucher & Partners project

The two leading competitors in the European market for specialty insulation were Morgan, based in the United Kingdom, and Continental Materials, based in Germany.[16] Morgan is the market leader in its home market, but has only a weak position in Germany, Europe's largest national market. Continental Materials (Conmat) faced the opposite situation. Both companies also trailed in France, where the domestic rival had by far the largest market share. Morgan also had a much stronger position than Conmat in Spain, but the Spanish market itself was considerably smaller than the other European markets.

When Morgan's growth stagnated, it didn't need to look far to find growth opportunities. It figured it had the best chances in expanding its position in the attractive German market. By now, you can easily guess what they made the core of their strategy: attack.

The company thought it could increase its market share from 8 percent to at least 15 percent, perhaps as high as 20 percent. It could subsidize the low prices because of the high profits earned in the less competitive and much more lucrative U.K. market. Morgan supported its price cuts in Germany by expanding its sales force and aggressively approaching customers.

Conmat had anticipated this kind of assault on its home market, where it had a 44 percent market share. It struck back immediately by cutting prices massively—not in Germany, but in the United Kingdom! Conmat had a small U.K. presence and thus little to lose. Morgan's assault changed the market's dynamics and forced Conmat to reevaluate its opportunities. Entering the UK market—an option it had always had available—now made more sense than ever. Just as Continental did to Northwest Airlines in the mid-1990s, Conmat figured that Morgan would feel the pain in its home market and would not take a softer signal seriously. Conmat thus focused its sales efforts almost entirely on Morgan's key accounts. It did not take long for Morgan to see just how it stood to lose. It stopped making price reductions in Germany.

Conmat had restored its balance in the German market and restored its prices in the United Kingdom to their previous levels. Morgan was fortunate that its attack—driven purely by price and price alone—did not do much permanent damage to its profit level.

Conmat had done its math and knew the dilemma it faced. Fighting Morgan directly in Germany instead of the United Kingdom would have been much riskier and expensive because it would have put more than three times as much business at risk as in the United Kingdom.

This equation has two sides. What did Morgan stand to lose? An attack in France or Spain would have not changed market dynamics sufficiently. It had little at risk in France and generated only 3 percent of its total sales there. It would have laughed off an attack in

Spain. The market was small to begin with, and Conmat's share of it tiny. It also felt it had little at risk in Germany, which motivated its "go for broke" pricing approach. Morgan, though, had everything to lose in its home market. The United Kingdom's profits paid the bills, and it could not take the risk of having those profits erode—probably forever—because of an unnecessary price war.

Learn to Receive and Interpret Signals

The easiest and best test of whether a signal is a signal is its relevance to your *customers*. That may appear strange at first glance. But as we mentioned in chapter 2, your focus should remain on your current and potential customers, not your competition. If the information a competitor communicates would have a direct impact on your own customers, assume it is a signal you should take seriously. You should then act accordingly and monitor subsequent responses. In the anecdote earlier in this chapter, the fact that Southwest sets its prices every Tuesday is on its own of no strategic relevance. The price levels, terms, and conditions it announces matter. Large, publicly traded corporations show considerable generosity with signaling their strategies, their revenue and profit projections, and their growth estimates for their industry.

You have seven dependable sources to monitor and send communications in your marketplace: your colleagues, governments, trade associations, analyst reports, local press reports, distributors, and customers. A financial analyst from a major brokerage house told one of the authors that he is always astonished at how much information CEOs and CFOs reveal in road shows and investor conferences.[17] The useful knowledge about your competitors is actually more soft than hard. The main question you need to focus on day in and day out is, How aggressive are your competitors? Are they minding their own business, or are they taking aggressive actions in the marketplace that will reduce your profits? To answer that question, you need to find and interpret the signals your competitors send.

The most powerful and meaningful signals, of course, are their actions. You need to observe what your competitors actually do in the marketplace and how it directly affects your customers. Only then can you see whether their actions line up with the strategies they may have outlined in their general market communications.

Most of those latter signals appear in the following sources, which are legal and which you can tap quickly.

- *Your own company.* Your colleagues all have their own collections of data, some of it hard and some of it unwritten and anecdotal. The challenge lies in structuring and evaluating that information. Most useful in assessing the mind-set of your competitors are obviously ex-employees of your customers who are now working for you.

- *Government data.* Chances are high that your competitor is a publicly traded company or is owned by one. In the United States, these companies must file detailed quarterly reports with the Securities and Exchange Commission (SEC). While much of the material in their annual reports (the 10-K or 20-F) is boilerplate or simply confirms what you already know, these reports do contain nuggets. The richest data usually lies buried in filings related to public offerings.

- *Trade associations.* Many of these groups pool data from members and play it back in summary form or in their own magazine. Others conduct market studies on behalf of their members, who could not afford this kind of research on their own.

- *Analyst reports.* Analysts participate in briefings, interviews, and other forms of research to compile their reports. The data they provide—whether inferred or quoted directly—goes into greater detail than official company reports and statements. Use them.

- *Local press.* You will also find valuable and often surprising information on competitors in the local press in the city or town where those companies operate. From these publications you get timely information on plant expansions or closings, changes in staffing, morale of the local employees, the results of approval processes for construction or zoning changes, and stray facts the company publicizes nowhere else.

- *Distributors and customers.* As far as launch plans, product advantages, and disadvantages are concerned, the actions of your customers and distributors will tell you everything you truly need to know. Spend more time tracking how *they* change, not your competitors.

Getting your market communication under control is the last piece that you need to defuse tension in your marketplace and capture the higher profits you deserve. By now you should have your assumptions, goals, and processes in alignment. Remember, though, that remaining consistent in your outward actions and statements is a crucial part of your "communication strategy."

Summary

The parties that make up your market—customers, competitors, analysts, regulators, and investors—are not mind readers. The only way they can understand and react to your company is to observe

201

your public actions and statements. That means you should pay careful attention to how the market will interpret your actions and especially your statements. These are the signals that help the market understand what you are thinking, what you are planning, and why you behave the way you do.

Failure to control your own public statements and actions systematically can make you appear inconsistent and unpredictable. You could encourage the market to respond in ways that undermine your profit rather than secure it.

You can make three kinds of signals: positive, neutral, and offensive. Positive signals help the market understand how you would respond to a specific change in the market. Neutral signals provide a general impression of your intentions. Offensive signals represent direct, unilateral responses to a competitor's actions. You use them when you have picked a fight worth winning. But before that, you need to be very specific in your communication that you have a natural space and you will defend it. We defined natural spaces when we introduced the competition map in chapter 2.

Everyone sends signals through their words and actions, not just you. Make sure you look for these signals in various media such as public filings, the business press, and the trade press. You should track and monitor these words and actions systematically and review them regularly.

CHAPTER 11

Epilogue—It's Time to Cash in
Your Profit Opportunities

IMPLEMENTING our program forces you to balance three commitments. You need to advocate the cultural change (reflected in the title of this book) that replaces aggression and acquiescence with a more appropriate form of competition built around differentiation and value. You need to encourage the rigor, discipline, and attention to detail required to undertake the program and monitor its progress. These first two commitments result in a third one: a commitment to deliver the anticipated financial results—the higher profits—that we have seen the companies described in this book produce.

Let's be realistic. None of this happens overnight. Contrary to our fondest hopes and dreams, this book will create controversy long before it ever creates consensus. When we say that our program can deliver a profit improvement equivalent to 1 to 3 percent of annual revenue to companies with mature products in mature markets, even the most skeptical managers take notice. They know their companies suffer from the global profit malaise we described in chapter 1. But they want proof and payback: show me how it can happen in *our* firm! And show me when *we* get our money!

We hope the cases in chapters 2 though 10 speak for themselves and provide you with relevant insights on how to establish proof in your own company and get the payback. Even if that's the case, however, you will probably have the same three requests that managers invariably have when they embark on this program:

- Tell me how to get started.

- Tell me what resources (people, money, time) I need to commit.

- Tell me what can go wrong.

We use most of this chapter to respond to those requests. We then provide you with a short list of questions you can use to characterize your current situation and measure the general direction and extent of your progress. Please keep in mind that most companies succeed with this program by creating expectations of progress rather than perfection. It is much more important to strive for steady progress—despite occasional setbacks—than to expect perfect results.

Stabilize Your Market Position, Then Redefine It

Chapters 2 and 3 showed how smart competitors earn higher profits by exercising restraint and by differentiating themselves through value (service, support, relationships, brand, etc.) rather than through aggressive prices. Peaceful competitors also rely on objective evidence and fact-based assumptions rather than on anecdotal evidence and industry conventional wisdom. These are powerful insights you need to translate into your own terms.

To begin this process, you need to start putting harder data into the competition map (chapter 2) and the profit curve (chapter 3). Again, progress is more important than perfection. Using the internal data analysis techniques described in chapter 4, most companies we work with quickly find enough egregious acts of aggression or acquiescence to demonstrate the negative effects.

You can then use this growing pile of evidence to launch an internal communication campaign to emphasize profit over market share. Without the evidence, you risk a setback because your team will perceive the statements as diatribes rather than something grounded in evidence and fact-based assumptions. In line with what we described in chapter 8, start taking a rigorous "guilty until proven innocent" approach with anyone who suggests taking an aggressive or acquiescent action (customer incentives, giveaways, exemptions from service and freight charges, price cuts, extended terms). Depending on the severity of your situation, this may force you to take more draconian control measures in the short term—such as stringent sign-off requirements on deals or penalties for noncompliance—in order to prevent profit-destroying behavior from continuing.

Because individual corporate cultures differ so greatly, it is hard for us to offer specific suggestions on how to communicate these measures. But we have observed that the maxim "The medium is the message" often applies. The mere threat of exposure, additional administrative burden, or penalties (earnings loss, poorer evaluations, loss of status) is often sufficient to compel sales and marketing people to start thinking through the consequences of their decisions and to start showing restraint. You should combine that threat, however, with an unequivocal policy that frees your organization from its most deep-seated fear: losing volume or, worse, losing a customer. Finally, you should praise and celebrate signs of real adoption—in word and deed—of this new mind-set.

The combination of this threat, the new policy, and the positive reinforcement will stabilize your situation by "stopping the bleeding." It will also help make people open to alternative approaches as your evidence—and your case for change—continues to grow. That evidence comes from the results you generate from the tools described in chapters 2 through 4. They will help you identify and counter weak or dubious assumptions, see clear indications of where you deliver more value than your competitors, and likewise see the first clear opportunities for extracting more value. They will provide you with the basis for your new market position, which will evolve as you work your way through the rest of the program.

Keep in mind the advice of Ted Levitt, who wrote that "sustained success is largely a matter of focusing regularly on the right things and making a lot of uncelebrated little improvements every day."[1] You will continually find room for improvement on your way from good profit performance to peak profit performance. The companies known as *hidden champions* serve as role models for this approach because they have realized that "good management means performing many minor details better than one's competitor rather than getting just one or a few elements right."[2]

Let Experienced Champions Lead the Effort

One personnel decision is critical for success: the choice of the internal champions for this effort. Convincing your company to focus on profit rather than market share—and tapping the resulting profit opportunities—will obviously demand involvement of C-level and senior executives. The chief marketing officer or chief financial officer usually shows the strongest affinity, but while they can take to the bully pulpit and reaffirm commitment, they cannot manage the day-to-day work.

That task should fall to an experienced manager with sales or marketing experience who has already lived through at least some market upheaval in his or her career. Such an upheaval could have been a period of severe over- or undercapacity, dramatic rises in raw material costs, a shakeout among customers or competitors, or a technological shift that forced the company to change the way it served its customers.

This profile might sound counterintuitive. Conventional wisdom says that most veteran managers per se would embody a "business as usual" mentality, make their decisions based solely on gut feeling, and harbor the greatest resistance to change. The longer they have been with the company, the more entrenched in their beliefs they would be.

This view is not only superficial, it also ignores several advantages that these managers have over younger colleagues who have had little or no disruptive change in their careers thus far. First, the upheaval in the past has already forced them to abandon conventional wisdom before, rather than extrapolate "business as usual" to the new situation. Conventional wisdom, as we said in chapter 3, becomes dangerous when the conditions in which it arose no longer apply.

Veteran managers can also bring their extensive personal experience with customers to bear in the internal exercises, such as the creation of demand curves, described in detail in chapter 4. As Peter Drucker points out, "no matter how good the reports, nothing beats personal, direct observation, and in a form in which it is truly outside observation."[3]

Finally, these managers can help challenge assumptions and conventional wisdom because they have the stature and power to ask dumb questions.[4] They can probe repeatedly by asking, "Why is that so?" and "What makes you so sure that that's what the customer really wants?"

Of course, you don't need to abandon the program if you cannot find someone with that exact profile in your organization. The next best candidate is someone who has years of experience working with customers, but also enjoys a good reputation and credibility among salespeople.

Executing this program will also require a monetary investment. As we explained in chapter 5, you need customer input in order to define your new marketing program (product, segmentation, promotion, price) optimally. While internal data can provide you with plenty of fresh insights, they are not always sufficient. In many cases, you will need to gather data directly from customers in order to test more sophisticated hypotheses. Valid external information is more difficult to come by and too often neglected in favor of internal information, a point repeatedly emphasized by Peter Drucker.[5] Therefore, this area requires specific attention and resource commitment from senior management. When a mature product can still yield tens of millions of dollars in additional profit, a six-figure investment in customer research seems very reasonable in order to ensure that you reach the optimum.

When a small company or division cannot justify that expense relative to the profit potential, it should still find some form of input from current and potential customers to serve as a proxy. We described some of these small-scale approaches in chapter 5 as well. No matter what the situation, customer input on preferences and willingness to pay is indispensable in designing products, developing bundles, setting prices, or planning promotions with profit in mind. Treat the collection of external customer data as an investment rather than an expense. A continual investment will enable your company to continue to fine-tune the marketing mix in order to tap additional profit opportunities and minimize the risk of adverse effects, especially an overreaction by customers, competitors, or investors.

The question of timing is the most difficult one to answer definitively. Because of the intensity of their commitment, some companies have seen their business stabilize and the "bleeding" stop in a matter of weeks, though a complete overview often takes three months to compile. This first milestone not only makes the initial profit opportunities accessible, it also builds buy-in and creates an appetite for the longer-term parts of the process: the lasting cultural change and the customer-driven changes to the marketing mix. Depending on the breadth of the insights and the need for adjustment, implementation delivers profit improvement but still takes a year to complete in full.

As for the lasting cultural change, this depends on the size of your organization and how you approach the program. Most companies we work with start with pilot projects (in one region or several) in order to establish proof and payback before exposing the rest of the organization. For a diversified, global *Fortune* 500 company, this process can take two to three years to reach every corner of the company.

Avoid Backsliding and Miscommunication

The three major pitfalls correspond to chapters 8 through 10. This program runs its greatest risks when a perceived setback—such as unexpectedly large loss of market share—causes some people to question their commitment to the effort. In chapter 8, we discussed many ways that people can undermine the program.

The challenge with incentives (see chapter 9) lies in convincing people to start adopting more profitable behaviors and practices before you have had the opportunity to change their official incentives. This is an unfortunate and often unavoidable nuisance because companies almost always launch this program during a fiscal year, after managers and employees have already agreed on individual incentives and objectives. The next opportunity for wholesale change is usually the start of the next fiscal year. You can best use the intervening weeks or months working with sales and marketing to reach agreement on new incentives, as described in chapter 9. The celebration of success in the course of the program, as mentioned earlier in this chapter, is a way to bridge the gap before a new system takes hold.

In conceiving a new system, you should try to ensure that salespeople and management fully understand the requirements and the rewards, and that information and rewards flow timely. Ideally, the salesperson can see the level of reward during the sale or negotiation, as in the system Kinston instituted (see chapter 9). The rewards should also be paid in short intervals (monthly is better than quarterly, quarterly is better than semiannually, etc.).

Finally, you need to manage the story about this change carefully. Mistakes or misinterpretations cause the most damage when

- Your customers see inconsistencies as a sign of weakness or lack of commitment and take advantage of that in negotiations

- Your competitors mistake your unilateral words or actions as a declaration of war (and then respond aggressively)

- Your sales force senses discrepancies between public and internal words and actions, and reverts to whatever system and tactics it previously used

The most cautious way is to treat every communication to the market—and every action your company takes—as a clear signal that leaves little room for misinterpretation. Having the courage and conviction to take consistent and conscious public actions is the final test of whether you have instilled a culture based on profit, restraint, and differentiation rather than a culture of aggression, acquiescence, and convenience.

Make Your Preparations: Where Does Your Business Stand Today?

We end the book with a brief set of questions that will allow you to track the progress you have made and define your urgent priorities in the pursuit of profit. Rate your company on a scale of 1 to 5, where 5 is the highest or best score:

- To what degree does senior management emphasize profit goals over market share goals?

- To what degree is your company prepared to trade lower volumes for higher profits?

- To what degree are all employees explicitly—and implicitly—rewarded for pursuing profit goals, not volume or market share ones?

- To what degree does your organization think through the consequences of marketing decisions by quantifying the effects they will have on profit?

- To what degree is your organization prepared to pursue peak profit performance, not just good performance?

- How good is your understanding of what drives differences in willingness to pay among your customer segments?

- To what degree have you avoided profit-destroying actions such as price cuts and value attacks?

- To what degree is your market communication—in word and deed—consciously planned to support efforts to preserve or increase profit?

The closer you get to a score of 40, the closer you should be to fulfilling to the promise of this book. You are more likely to find and tap a profit opportunity equivalent to 1 to 3 percent of your annual revenue. This can translate into millions of dollars of additional profit. You should be able to achieve that profit with the same people and the same mature products you have today. Finally, you should be able to achieve that profit gain by staying true to the integrated program of many small actions described in this book, rather than looking for the one big idea. The data in figure 1-1 in chapter 1 showed that U.S. companies have a profit margin of 4.1 percent. Adding 1 to 3 percentage points to that figure would indeed be a profit renaissance.

Notes

CHAPTER 1

1. David Sedgwick, "Market Share Meltdown," *Automotive News*, November 4, 2002.

2. "GM Is Still Studying the $100,000 Cadillac," *Automotive News*, May 17, 2004.

3. For an empirical confirmation, see David Ogilvy, *Ogilvy on Advertising* (New York: Vintage Books, 1983), 74.

4. *Standort Deutschland—Ein internationaler Vergleich* (Cologne: Institut der deutschen Wirtschaft, 2005).

5. Robert D. Buzzell and Bradley T. Gale, *The PIMS Principles: Linking Strategy to Performance* (New York: Free Press, 1987), 94.

6. Bruce D. Henderson, *Perspectives on Experience* (Boston: Boston Consulting Group, 1968).

7. See, for example, Robert Jacobson and David A. Aaker, "Is Market Share All That It's Cracked Up to Be?" *Journal of Marketing* 49 (Fall 1985).

8. Paul W. Farris and Michael J. Moore, *The Profit Impact of Marketing Strategy Project: Retrospect and Prospects* (Cambridge: Cambridge University Press, 2003). ✓

9. Kusum L. Ailawadi, Paul W. Farris, and Mark E. Parry, "Market Share and ROI: Observing the Effect of Unobserved Variables," *International Journal of Research in Marketing* 16 (1999): 17–33.

10. Ibid.

11. Robert F. Lanzillotti, "Pricing Objectives in Large Companies," *American Economic Review* 48 (1958): 921–40.

12. J. Scott Armstrong and Kesten C. Green, "Competitor-oriented Objectives: The Myth of Market Share," working paper, September 26, 2005.

13. Starbucks Web site: www.starbucks.com.

14. Starbucks 10-K filing, February 18, 2005.

15. For more detailed information, see Richard Harmer and Leslie L. Simmel, "How Much Market Share Is Too Much?" working paper, CustomerValueCenter LLC, 2001–2003.

16. Details of this case have been modified to protect confidentiality.

17. Details of this case have been modified to protect confidentiality.

18. W. Chan Kim and Renée Mauborgne, *Blue Ocean Strategy: How to Create Uncontested Market Space and Make the Competition Irrelevant* (Boston: Harvard Business School Press, 2005).

19. Daniel Goleman, Richard Boyatzis, and Annie McKee, "Primal Leadership: The Hidden Driver of Great Performance," *Harvard Business Review*, December 2001.

CHAPTER 2

1. Friedrich von Hayek, *The Counter-Revolution of Science* (Glencoe, IL: The Free Press, 1952), 105.

2. Details of this case have been altered to protect confidentiality.

3. Richard Harmer and Leslie L. Simmel, "How Much Market Share Is Too Much?" working paper, CustomerValueCenter LLC, 2001–2003, 1.

4. Ibid.

5. Rainer Meckes and Felix Krohn, "Lessons from the Decline of the House of Reuters," *Wall Street Journal Europe*, December 2, 2002.

6. Ajay Kalra, Surenda Rajiv, and Kannan Srinivasan, "Response to Competitive Entry: A Rationale for Delayed Defensive Reaction," *Marketing Science* 17, no. 4 (1998): 383.

7. Details of this case have been altered to protect confidentiality.

CHAPTER 3

1. Discussion with one of the authors, February 2003.

2. Konrad P. Koerding and Daniel M. Wolpert, "Bayesian Integration in Sensorimotor Learning," *Nature* 427 (2004): 244–247.

3. Charles Roxburgh, "Hidden Flaws in Strategy," *McKinsey Quarterly* 2 (2003).

4. Details of this case have been altered to protect confidentiality.

5. Details of this case have been altered to protect confidentiality.

6. Susanne Wied-Nebbeling, *Das Preisverhalten in der Industrie* (Tuebingen: Mohr-Siebeck, 1985), 137.

7. Robert J. Dolan and Hermann Simon, *Power Pricing* (New York: Free Press, 1996), 37.

8. Ibid., 37–38.

9. Thomas T. Nagle and Reed K. Holden, *The Strategy and Tactics of Pricing*, 2nd ed. (Upper Saddle River, NJ: Prentice Hall, 1995), 3.

10. Neal E. Boudette, "Power Play: Chrysler's Storied Hemi Motor Helps It Escape Detroit's Gloom," *Wall Street Journal*, June 17, 2005.

11. Andy Serwer, "Inside the Rolling Stones Inc.," *Fortune*, September 30, 2002.

12. Frank F. Bilstein and Frank Luby, "Don't Price Away Your Profits," *Wall Street Journal Europe*, September 23, 2002.

CHAPTER 4

1. Fred Vogelstein, "Mighty Amazon," *Fortune*, May 26, 2003.

2. John D. C. Little, "Decision Support Systems for Marketing Managers," *Journal of Marketing* 43 (July 1979).

3. Details of this case have been altered to protect confidentiality.

4. Peter Rossi, Phil DeLurgio, and David Kantor, "Making Sense of Scanner Data," *Harvard Business Review*, March–April 2000, 24.

5. Faith Keenan, "The Price Is Really Right," *BusinessWeek*, March 31, 2003.

6. Ibid.

7. Details of this case have been altered to protect confidentiality.

8. Details of this case have been altered to protect confidentiality.

CHAPTER 5

1. Michael Lewis, *Moneyball: The Art of Winning an Unfair Game* (New York: W.W. Norton & Company, 2003), 98.

2. Details of this case have been altered to protect confidentiality.

3. Details of this case have been altered to protect confidentiality.

4. For a more detailed treatment, see Paul E. Green and V. Srinivasan, "Conjoint Analysis in Consumer Research: New Developments and Directions," *Journal of Marketing* 54 (October 1999); or Dick McCullough, "A User's Guide to Conjoint Analysis," *Marketing Research* 14, no. 2 (Summer 2002): 19.

5. David Ogilvy, *Ogilvy on Advertising* (New York: Vintage Books, 1985), 164.

6. Hermann Simon, *Hidden Champions: Lessons from 500 of the World's Best Unknown Companies* (Boston: Harvard Business School Press, 1996), 137–138.

7. Details of this case have been altered to protect confidentiality.

8. Details of this case have been altered to protect confidentiality.

CHAPTER 6

1. Steven D. Levitt and Stephen J. Dubner, *Freakonomics: A Rogue Economist Explores the Hidden Side of Everything* (New York: William Morrow, 2005), 14.

2. Details of this case have been altered to protect confidentiality.

3. Chris Zook, *Beyond the Core: Expand the Market Without Abandoning Your Roots* (Boston: Harvard Business School Press, 2004), 3–5.

4. Ralph Fuerderer, Andreas Herrmann, and Georg Wuebker, *Optimal Bundling: Marketing Strategies for Improving Economic Performance* (Berlin: Springer Verlag, 1999), 25.

5. Ibid.

6. Details of this case have been altered to protect confidentiality.

7. Details of this case have been altered to protect confidentiality.

8. Claude C. Hopkins, *My Life in Advertising* and *Scientific Advertising* (Lincolnwood, IL: NTC Business Books, 1986), 266.

9. Scott A. Neslin, "ROI Analysis of Pharmaceutical Promotions (RAPP): An Independent Study," unpublished presentation, May 22, 2001, 15.

CHAPTER 7

1. Hermann Simon, "Pricing Becomes a Science," *Financial Times*, October 31, 2000.

2. Richard Harmer and Leslie L. Simmel, "How Much Market Share Is Too Much?" working paper, CustomerValueCenter LLC, 2001–2003, 1.

3. Details of this case have been altered to protect confidentiality.

4. We would like to note that despite this praise, we have always been critical of America Online's single-minded obsession with flat-rate pricing. See the commentary by Markus Kreusch and Frank Luby, "The Flat-Rate Fallacy," *Wall Street Journal Europe*, May 13, 2001.

5. Frank F. Bilstein and Frank Luby, "Casing AOL's Flat-Price Model," *Wall Street Journal*, December 10, 2002.

6. Data on the salaries of Major League Baseball players is available from many sources, including ESPN.com.

7. Conversation with Frank Luby, Toronto, March 2003.

8. Vicki L. James, "Build Fan Base from Your Database," *Sports Business Journal*, June 14–20, 2004.

9. Dave Feschuk, "Market-Savvy Jays Discover the Winning Ticket," *Toronto Star*, February 6, 2004.

10. Ran Kivetz, Oded Netzer, and V. Srinivasan, "Alternative Models ✓ for Capturing the Compromise Effect," *Journal of Marketing Research* XLI (August 2004): 237–257.

CHAPTER 8

1. John D. C. Little, "Decision Support Systems for Marketing Managers," *Journal of Marketing* 43 (July 1979).

2. Peter F. Drucker, *The Practice of Management* (New York: Harper-Collins Publishers, 1954).

3. Stephan A. Butscher and Frank Luby, "The Real Toy Story," *Wall Street Journal Europe*, January 28, 2002.

4. Andreas Kraemer, Robert Bongartz, and Armin Weber, "Rabattsysteme und Bonusprogramme," in *Handbuch Preispolitik*, eds. *Hermann Diller and Andreas Hermann* (Wiesbaden, Germany: Gabler-Verlag, 2002), 560.

5. "Frequent-Flyer Economics," *Economist*, May 2, 2002.

6. Megan Johnston, "Frequent Flier Alert," *CNN Money*, December 5, 2003, http://money.cnn.com/2003/12/04/pf/frequent_flier/.

7. "US Airways Implements Pricing Changes," US Airways press release, August 27, 2002.

8. Barbara De Lollis, "Mileage Incident Bugs Some US Airways Fliers," *USA Today*, January 27, 2003.

9. Keith L. Alexander, "'Cockroaches' US Airways Worked to Keep," *Washington Post*, August 24, 2004.

10. Werner Reinartz and V. Kumar, "The Mismanagement of Customer Loyalty," *Harvard Business Review*, July 2002. ✓

11. Details of this case have been altered to protect confidentiality.

12. Ethan Smith, "Universal Slashes Its CD Prices in Bid to Revive Music Industry," *Wall Street Journal*, September 4, 2003.

13. Brian Carney, "Price Cuts Can't Save the Music Business," *Wall Street Journal Europe*, September 22, 2003.

14. David Kirkpatrick, "CD Price Cuts Could Mean New Artists Will Suffer," *New York Times*, September 20, 2003.

15. Ethan Smith, "Universal Slashes Its CD Prices in Bid to Revive Music Industry," *Wall Street Journal*, September 4, 2003.

16. "2002 Consumer Profile," Recording Industry Association of America (RIAA), Washington, DC.

17. Ethan Smith, "Music Industry Sounds Upbeat as Losses Slow," *Wall Street Journal*, January 2, 2004.

18. Ethan Smith, "Why a Grand Plan to Cut CD Prices Went off the Track," *Wall Street Journal*, June 4, 2004.

19. Janet Whitman, "Sony Aims to Improve Ties Between Products, Services," *Wall Street Journal*, November 5, 2003.

20. "Wiedeking's Strategy for Porsche: Image Builds Business," *Automotive News*, November 18, 2002.

21. Diana T. Kurylko, "Porsche Again Offers Incentives," *Automotive News*, November 2002.

CHAPTER 9

1. Discussion with one of the authors, May 2003.
2. Details of this case have been altered to protect confidentiality.
3. Details of this case have been altered to protect confidentiality.
4. Details of this case have been altered to protect confidentiality.
5. Details of this case have been altered to protect confidentiality.
6. Carlos Tejada and Gary McWilliams, "In a Tight Market, Employers Are Finding Job Seekers Willing to Take Lower Salaries," *Wall Street Journal*, February 5, 2003.
7. Ibid.

CHAPTER 10

1. Norihiko Shirouzu, "Redesigned Ford F-150 Pickup May Launch with Discounts," *Wall Street Journal*, February 18, 2003.

2. Taska Mazaroli, "Siemens Wants to Match Nokia Cuts But Wants to Avoid Price War," *Wall Street Journal*, June 18, 2004.

3. Pui-Wing Tam, "H-P Gains by Ceding Market Share to Dell," *Wall Street Journal*, January 18, 2005.

4. Michael E. Porter, *Competitive Strategy* (New York: Free Press, 1984), 75.

5. Scott McCartney, "Logic Behind Air Fares Often Defies Economics," WSJ.com, October 1, 2003.

6. Shirouzu, "Redesigned Ford F-150 Pickup May Launch with Discounts."

7. Norihiko Shirouzu, "Ford and GM Gear Up for Price War on Trucks," *Wall Street Journal*, July 2, 2003.

8. Ibid.

9. Russ Banham, "The Right Price," *CFO Magazine*, October 2003.

10. "IKEA muss neue Konkurrenten abwehren," *Frankfurter Allgemeine Zeitung*, April 5, 2003.

11. "Aggressive Ryanair Keeps Soaring,"*CNN.com*, June 3, 2003.

12. "Ryanair will Preise senken," *Frankfurter Allgemeine Zeitung*, April 22, 2003.

13. Quotations in figure 10-1 come from the following sources: Cecily Barnes, Jim Hu, and Larry Dignan, "Case: Rate Hike 'in the Cards' for AOL Service," CNet news.com, January 31, 2001; Daniel DeLong, "AOL-MSN Clash Begins with War of Words," *NewsFactor Network*, February 14, 2001; John Yaukey, "AOL Won't Raise Rates in Short Term," *Gannett News Service*, April 30, 2001.

14. "Tust du mir nichts, tue ich Dir nichts," *Frankfurter Allgemeine Zeitung*, June 16, 2003.

15. "Big Airlines Take Another Run at a Fare Increase," *New York Times*, February 18, 2003.

16. Details of this case have been altered to protect confidentiality.

17. Conversation with Hermann Simon, January 2005.

CHAPTER 11

1. Theodore Levitt, "Betterness," *Harvard Business Review*, November–December 1988, 9.

2. Hermann Simon, *Hidden Champions: Lessons from 500 of the World's Best Unknown Companies* (Boston: Harvard Business School Press, 1996), 271.

3. Peter Drucker, *Management Challenges for the 21st Century* (New York: Harper Business, 1999), 130.

4. See a good discussion of this topic in Geoffrey Colvin, "The Wisdom of Dumb Questions," *Fortune*, June 27, 2005, 54.

5. Drucker, *Management Challenges for the 21st Century*, 101.

Acknowledgments

When we began this project in 2002, we did not fully realize the extent of collaborative guidance required to bring it to fruition. We extend our heartfelt thanks to everyone who kept us headed in the right direction, but especially to a select few.

Joshua Bloom, a senior consultant in Simon-Kucher & Partners' Boston office, served as our shadow editor and continually provided constructive feedback. Andrew Conrad and Cory Polonetsky, likewise based in our Boston office, provided valuable insights that helped us structure the book. We also thank our partner and colleague Georg Wuebker in Zurich for his help with the sections on bundling. Ingo Lier and Dorothea Hayer managed the documentation and information flow professionally in Bonn, as did Matt Weisinger in Boston.

In the opening chapter, we noted that "profit versus market share" attracts not only management attention, but also academic attention, inspired in part by a healthy skepticism over the famous PIMS findings. We thank Richard Harmer, Leslie Simmel, J. Scott Armstrong, and Kesten C. Green for their insights and for the permission to cite their papers in our book.

We are indebted to the entire team at Harvard Business School Press, in particular the editors with whom we worked most closely. Executive editor Kirsten Sandberg kept the project's momentum going, even when our progress slowed. Developmental editor Ann Goodsell's input gave rise to the book's ultimate structure and flow. Assistant editor Julia Ely's contributions became even more important as the manuscript entered its final stages.

Speaking of editors, we thank Brian Carney, a member of the editorial board of the *Wall Street Journal*, and Therese Raphael, a former editorial page editor for its European edition. Their critical comments and copious feedback to our commentaries on marketing, profit, and pricing helped us find our voice and strengthened our confidence.

Of course, we thank our clients around the world for allowing us to serve as their partners over the last twenty years. Their successes, based on their own commitment to ideas and implementation, will always remain the true proof of the concepts and the program in this book.

Finally, we feel honored and humbled that the late Peter F. Drucker took enough interest in our project to follow its development and actively offer suggestions and ongoing guidance. Echoing Joseph Schumpeter's theories of economic development and creative destruction, he once wrote that economics should treat profit as a genuine cost, the cost of staying in business. Profit, he argued, enables rapid technological change, productivity growth, and job creation. To help us and our readers better interpret the meaning of profit orientation, Drucker cautioned us that we should emphasize the importance of sustainable high profits, not short-term profit maximization for its own sake. One week before he passed away in November 2005, he sent us a succinct summary of his views on our completed manuscript, which we had sent to him one month earlier: "I have always emphasized that market share and profitability have to be balanced and that profitability has often been neglected in the rush toward market share. Your book is therefore a greatly needed correction."

With the utmost respect, we dedicate our book to the memory of Peter Drucker.

Hermann Simon
Frank F. Bilstein
Frank Luby

Index

About the Authors

Hermann Simon is the founder and chairman of Simon-Kucher & Partners Strategy and Marketing Consultants. He is a leading strategy, marketing, and pricing expert who continues to consult to clients around the world. Hermann has published more than thirty books, including the bestsellers *Hidden Champions*, *Power Pricing*, and *Think!* He has also contributed to leading business and academic publications, including *Harvard Business Review*, *Management Science*, the *Financial Times*, and the *Wall Street Journal*.

In his "first" life, Hermann served as a professor for management science and marketing at the universities in Mainz and Bielefeld. He has also served as a visiting professor at numerous institutions, including Harvard Business School, Stanford University, INSEAD, the Massachusetts Institute of Technology, London Business School, and Keio-University Tokyo.

Frank F. Bilstein is a partner with Simon-Kucher & Partners. He originally joined the firm in 1997 and most recently served as managing director of the Boston office. He is a frequent speaker at national and international conferences and the author of several publications on general management, marketing, and pricing. His commentaries have appeared in the *Wall Street Journal* and other leading publications.

His experience also included two years as chief marketing officer of a B2C e-commerce company in Germany and two years as a project manager for a predecessor company of Sanofi-Aventis in Germany and Japan. Frank studied business administration at the WHU Graduate School of Management, the University of Washington, and the University of Kobe (Japan), and also has a degree in literature.

Frank Luby is a partner with Simon-Kucher & Partners. He has over two decades of experience as a consultant and journalist in the United States and in Europe. His writings and comments on marketing and pricing have been published in the *Wall Street Journal*, *Financial Times*, *Advertising Age*, and numerous other leading business publications.

Prior to joining Simon-Kucher & Partners in 1996, he spent four years as a financial news editor. He began his consulting career with the economic consulting firms Lexecon and Analysis Group, and has also worked as a freelance journalist and editor. He holds a degree in physics from the University of Chicago.